'RACE', ETHNICITY AND ADOPTION

'RACE', HEALTH AND SOCIAL CARE

Series editors:

Professor Waqar I.U. Ahmad, Professor of Primary Care Research and Director, Centre for Research in Primary Care, University of Leeds.

Professor Charles Husband, Professor of Social Analysis and Director, Ethnicity and Social Policy Research Unit (ESPR), University of Bradford.

Minority ethnic groups now constitute over 5 per cent of the UK population. While research literature has mushroomed on the one hand in race and ethnic relations generally, and on the other in clinical and epidemiological studies of differences in conditions and use of health and social services, there remains a dearth of credible social scientific literature on the health and social care of minority ethnic communities. Social researchers have hitherto largely neglected issues of 'race' and ethnicity, while acknowledging the importance of gender, class and, more recently, (dis)ability in both the construction of and provision for health and social care needs. Consequently the available social science texts on health and social care largely reflect the experiences of the white population and have been criticized for marginalizing minority ethnic people.

This series aims to provide an authoritative source of policy relevant texts which specifically address issues of health and social care in contemporary multi-ethnic Britain. Given the rate of change in the structure of health and social care services, demography and the political context of state welfare there is a need for a critical appraisal of the health and social care needs of, and provision for, the minority ethnic communities in Britain. By the nature of the issues we will address, this series will draw upon a wide range of professional and academic expertise, thus enabling a deliberate and necessary integration of theory and practice in these fields. The books will be interdisciplinary and written in clear, non-technical language which will appeal to a broad range of students, academics and professionals with a common interest in 'race', health and social care.

Current and forthcoming titles
Waqar I.U. Ahmad: *Ethnicity, Disability and Caring*
Waqar I.U. Ahmad and Karl Atkin: *'Race' and Community Care*
Elizabeth Anionwu and Karl Atkin: *The Politics of Sickle Cell and Thalassaemia – 20 Years On*
Kate Gerrish, Charles Husband and Jennifer Mackenzie: *Nursing for a Multi-ethnic Society*
Savita Katbamna: *'Race' and Childbirth*
Derek Kirton: *'Race', Ethnicity and Adoption*
Lena Robinson: *'Race', Communication and the Caring Professions*

'RACE', ETHNICITY AND ADOPTION

Derek Kirton

Open University Press
Buckingham · Philadelphia

Open University Press
Celtic Court
22 Ballmoor
Buckingham
MK18 1XW

email: enquiries@openup.co.uk
world wide web: http://www.openup.co.uk

and
325 Chestnut Street
Philadelphia, PA 19106, USA

First Published 2000

A catalogue record of this book is available from the British Library

ISBN   0 335 20003 6 (hb)   0 335 20002 8 (pb)

Library of Congress Cataloging-in-Publication Data
Kirton, Derek.
  'Race', ethnicity, and adoption / Derek Kirton.
    p.   cm. – (Race, health, and social care)
  Includes bibliographical references and index.
  ISBN 0-335-20003-6 (hardbound). – ISBN 0-335-20002-8 (pbk.)
  1. Adoption – Great Britain.   2. Interracial adoption – Great
Britain.   3. Children of minorities – Great Britain.   4. Racism –
Great Britain.   5. Ethnicity – Great Britain.   6. Adoption – United
States.   7. Interracial adoption – United States.   8. Children of
minorities – United States.   9. Racism – United States.
10. Ethnicity – United States.   I. Title.   II. Series.
HV875.58.G7K57   2000
362.273'4'0941–dc21   99–41020
                                                                CIP

Typeset by Graphicraft Limited, Hong Kong
Printed in Great Britain by St Edmundsbury Press Ltd,
Bury St Edmunds, Suffolk

To Linda, Anna and Betty
and the memory of Lyn and Tom

Contents

Acknowledgements

As with most books, the gestation period for this volume has been a long one, with several years as a writer and researcher on 'race', ethnicity and adoption preceded by several more as a child care practitioner. During that time, countless people have contributed to the ideas set out here, albeit some in ways they may not recognize or approve. In terms of the writing of the book, I would particularly like to thank Charles Husband, Felicity Collier, Marie McNay and Joan Fletcher for their helpful comments on draft material; Sue Jardine and David Woodger for their support; and all those adoptees, excerpts of whose interviews appear in Chapter 4. I would also like to thank Jacinta Evans, Joan Malherbe and Maureen Cox from Open University Press for guiding me patiently through the publishing process.

The message of this book is that the past two decades have seen great advances in the welfare of minority ethnic children but that there remains much to be done. My final acknowledgement is to all those involved in adoption and foster care, black and white, who have helped bring about the changes and who continue the struggle 'in a cold climate'.

Introduction: 'race', ethnicity and adoption

Policy and practice relating to the adoption of black and minority ethnic children has been one of the most contentious aspects of child care in Britain and the United States for over three decades. Protracted, often bitter, struggles have been fought among those who would claim to have the children's best interests at heart. The conflicts have taken place in varied arenas, mostly relatively private, but sometimes in the full glare of media publicity. At the centre of debate lies the phenomenon of transracial adoption (TRA), its perceived merits and flaws. The primary source of contention is that it is taking place in a racially divided and race-conscious society. Thus, beneath the apparent neutrality of the language, TRA has historically represented a form of 'one-way traffic', with black and minority ethnic children moving to white homes. Such passages have attracted critical attention, focusing on questions of racialized power and its significance for both interpersonal relationships and wider social processes. While the arguments deployed are both varied and complex, they have tended to crystallize around levels of support for or opposition to TRA, the extent to which it is desirable and, if so, in what circumstances?

This book seeks to explore the struggles which have taken place over 'race', ethnicity and adoption, their history and focal points. The question of sources for such an endeavour reveals something of a paradox. On the one hand, there is a substantial literature. As early as the mid-1980s, a bibliography compiled by Harris (1985) showed over 370 relevant entries. Yet, as will be argued here, there remain major gaps in our knowledge. One of the most obvious areas of ignorance surrounds the numbers of children adopted transracially or inter-country in Britain (or in recent years in the United States). In spite of, or perhaps because of, the contentiousness of the area, there has been no official ethnic monitoring either of children in the public care system or of those adopted. (The Labour government in the UK has, however, pledged to introduce ethnic monitoring in the near future.) In its absence, we are left to rely on a few snapshot pictures emerging either from research or localized monitoring. More importantly, insights into the lived experiences of adoptees and their families remain limited, as do those into the practices of social work agencies. If it is true that more information can often simply mean more to squabble over, it is also plausible that the gaps in our knowledge have contributed to the ferocity of debate while hindering its quality.

The atmosphere within which battles over 'race', ethnicity and adoption have been fought is a highly charged one, attributable to the intersection of two already charged domains. Adoption raises questions of the needs of children, of what constitutes adequate parenting, of circumstances under which substitute parenting is preferable to the 'blood tie', of the suitability of substitute parents and the nature of the transfer involved. It has often been observed that adoption has a resonance much wider than its apparently small scale.[1] At the (inter)personal level, it touches on powerful questions of identity, nature and nurture, family loyalties, separation and loss. The fictional fascination with identities lost and found bears witness to this power (Reich 1992; Mosse 1996; Leigh 1997). The links between adoption and childlessness have long been acknowledged, while more belatedly recognition has been given to the traumatic effects of giving up a child for adoption. The circumstances leading to adoption highlight a wider social and political significance. While the social stigma attached to illegitimacy has declined dramatically, adoption customarily remains for the children a form of social mobility, from relatively poor families to the more affluent (Mandell 1973; Holman 1978). This movement can be viewed benignly – a product of altruism which is best for all concerned – or as a cynical and punitive form of 'child-snatching' sponsored by the state. Adoption is thus inextricably bound up with notions of social justice, whether at the level of contested cases (Ryburn 1994a) or debate on the desirability or necessity of adoption itself. Moreover, as the recent debates on the age, sexual orientation, marital status and even smoking habits of prospective adopters have shown, suitability to adopt is closely linked with a wider politics of the family.

When adoption is linked to issues of 'race', it connects with the diversity and complexity of debates on racial justice. 'Race' is clearly relevant to all the issues outlined above, from the nature of identity and heritage, family life, or the lived experiences of a race-conscious society through to more abstracted political questions of racial integration, harmony and equality. Above all, it raises profound questions about the needs of minority ethnic children and the capacities of families, ethnically matched or not, to meet them. If adoption is already primed for public controversy, it is its articulation with issues of 'race' and ethnicity which lights the touch paper (Kirton 1992).

The aims of this book are to provide an examination of the arguments which have been brought to bear on these issues and to set out the author's own position on 'race', ethnicity and adoption. A key element in this exercise is to locate debates in their wider political context(s). While this will draw primarily on social science-based theory and research, some material will also be included from interviews undertaken with transracially adopted adults, these in turn being part of wider, ongoing research.[2]

Although the major focus of analysis rests with 'domestic' adoption in Britain, we will also be considering parallel debates in the United States. This is partly for comparative purposes but also in recognition of the trans-atlantic influences stemming from developments in the US. Debates on inter-country adoption (ICA) will also be touched upon, not least because such adoption is almost invariably transcultural and usually transracial and therefore offers another valuable source for comparison.

After an opening historical chapter, the book is broadly divided into two parts. The first, comprising Chapters 2 to 4, looks at debates on 'race', ethnicity and adoption as they impact on individual children and families. The primary focus will be on issues of identity, culture and coping with racism, which will be considered through three paradigms – namely those rooted in liberalism, black radicalism and post-modernism. In Chapter 4, the author's own position will be set out in response to the challenges posed by post-structuralist analyses. The second part examines the links between adoption and its wider contexts, namely those of the child care system (Chapter 5) and competing visions of society (Chapter 6).

Some notes on terminology

For a book with 'race' and ethnicity in its title, it is appropriate to offer some comment on their usage. Common to the many variable definitions of '*race*' is the use of (quasi) biological characteristics – most notably skin colour, but also hair or facial features – as a way of categorizing people. Importantly, this has also served as a means of attribution – by which to read off a range of other characteristics, so that 'races' become associated with particular qualities, capacities and proclivities. In the history of race-thinking, the latter have often been naturalized, deemed inherent attributes of the 'race' concerned. In more social versions of 'race', the quasi-biological serves as a marker for a socio-political process of attribution. Crucial to understanding the concept of 'race' are its profound paradoxes. Notwithstanding the efforts of a few flat earthers, doggedly exploring the intellectual inferiority or natural rhythm and athletic prowess of black populations, the notion that 'races' exist in any meaningful scientific sense has been widely discredited and largely abandoned (Montagu 1964; Banton 1977). Among other things, this has led to the convention, followed here, of placing the term race within inverted commas. Yet few social commentators, expert or lay, would dispute the continuing power exerted by the idea of 'race' and its attendant practices. It thus emerges as a concept which is simultaneously meaningful and meaningless. As Malik observes, 'everyone knows, but no-one can define', going on to note that 'western society seems to be repelled by the consequence of racial thinking yet forced to accept its importance' (1996: 2).

In academic literature, the term *racialization* has increasingly been used as a way of overcoming some of the difficulties presented by the concept of 'race' (Small 1994). This can be seen as an attempt to move further from any idea that 'races' exist and, instead, to switch attention to the processes through which ideas about 'race' originate and develop historically. Thus, racialization usually refers to those processes whereby 'race' as a supposedly real phenomenon is introduced into a description of the world; and is then drawn upon to explain that world. A focus on racialization opens up various useful avenues of enquiry. These include how particular groups come to be racialized, regarded as and treated as a 'race' – perhaps the most powerful historical example being that of European racialization of Africans. How are the boundaries of racialized categories drawn, maintained or changed – who is to be regarded as white, black and so forth and upon what basis? How do particular attributes become linked to racialized groups? What are the consequences of racialization in terms of discrimination and inequality? Such questions allow investigation of meanings and practices associated with racialization, acknowledging their social and historical significance, but hopefully without entrenching belief in the existence of 'races'.

However, the paradoxes of 'race' still haunt those who aspire to racial justice and equality, creating sharp divisions on the best means to achieving them. Amid the many different stances taken, two broad positions can be identified. On the one hand, there are those who favour deracialization and see 'colour blindness' as the way forward. This position emphasizes the 'non-existence' of 'race' and hence the irrationality of those who believe in its importance. From such a perspective, the best prospects for tackling racism rest with playing down the significance of 'race' and allowing it to wither away, while giving it weight, for whatever reasons, is likely to exacerbate racialized divisions. On the other hand, there are those who contend that 'race' and racism are deeply embedded within western society and that deracialization only serves to obscure this reality. Far from being played down, the effects of racialization must be clearly recognized in order for them to be challenged. These competing perspectives have exerted a profound influence over debate on 'race', ethnicity and adoption and will be explored in greater detail in subsequent chapters.

Ethnicity is usually defined in ways which draw on two key elements, namely those of shared common descent and cultural heritage (including language, religion, customs, values etc.), as perceived by self and others. Malik casts ethnicity as a bridge between 'race' and culture while, speaking of minority groups in Britain, Mason refers to 'an unstable combination of skin colour and distinctive culture' as the definitive criterion or marker (1995: 16). The relationship between ethnicity and 'race' is complex and for various reasons it is not possible to maintain any neat and tidy distinction between them. Many of the processes involved in racialization are paralleled in those of 'ethnicization', as categories, boundaries and 'ethnic' attributes are struggled over and evolve. Both terms are used as bases for mobilization and are, in important ways, 'imagined communities'. Clear effect of class divisions on relationships between black workers and the wider black community. Initiatives such as the LCC's were rare. An early 1960s survey by the National Council for Civil Liberties found only five agencies attempting to place 'coloured' children and reported judges often refusing transracial placements on grounds akin to 'miscegenation' arguments (cited in Gaber 1994: 15).

More systematic efforts to find adoptive homes for black and minority ethnic children are usually traced to the work of the British Adoption Project (BAP), which also established transracial adoption as a 'recognized' phenomenon. More detailed aspects of the BAP will be considered in later chapters, but a brief overview is useful at this point. The project's establishment was first mooted in 1962, promoted by International Social Service of Great Britain, and recruitment activities commenced in 1965. Optimism over the adoptability of 'non-white' children had been boosted by the adoption of around 100 children from Hong Kong in the early 1960s (Bagley 1993: 152). By the mid-1960s, as the BAP's own survey demonstrated, adoption of non-white children was by no means rare, accounting for 3.4 per cent of agency adoptions nationally, and 7.5 per cent in London (Raynor 1970: 168). A clear majority of these, however, were adoptions by foster carers with whom the children had been placed, leaving the question of direct adoption more open. It was such direct recruitment which the BAP sought, and, as an action research project, the promotion of 'good practice' in this area.

It is interesting to note that in its original Memorandum, the BAP stated 'as a fundamental principle that children should be placed whenever possible with adoptive parents of the same racial background as themselves' (cited in Raynor 1970: 26). Equally clear, however, was the assumption that the 'whenever possible' might be severely limited, and that the majority of adopters would be white. As it transpired, roughly 20 per cent of families coming forward (and of those eventually adopting) had at least one 'non-white' member. For the white adopters, the profile of transracial adopters found in the United States (Grow and Shapiro 1974; Simon and Altstein 1977) was repeated, namely that adopters were drawn primarily from the 'liberal middle class', highly educated, though not generally very high earners, and living in predominantly white areas (Raynor 1970: 87–8). Most were already parents, their interest in adoption relatively new and specific to 'non-white' children (p. 92).

It is clear that the BAP saw its pioneering role as working in spite of a climate where prejudice was prevalent. Among criteria for (white) adopters was that they should have 'no more than a minimal amount of mild prejudice' (Raynor 1970: 68). Similarly, Raynor notes that the conflicts faced by many white workers in this field, who experienced feelings of racial prejudice while knowing them to be unacceptable, often led to 'denial' on 'race' issues (p. 77). Such openness gives a powerful indication of the extent to which prejudice remained a naturalized phenomenon. Yet there is also an eerie silence on the question of prejudice. In spite of the above criterion, we are given no indication of even mild prejudices among those accepted as adopters, while prejudice does not appear anywhere among reasons given for rejection (p. 94). This coupling of abstract recognition with concrete denial tells us much about racialized discourse at the time.

What is clear from Raynor's work is that the BAP was as much about the establishment of transracial adoption as finding homes for specific children. She is quite clear about its achievements on both counts, combining 'successful' placements with the establishment of the Adoption Resource Exchange to coordinate future placements. Transracial adoption was given its official blessing in the Home Office's *Guide to Adoption Practice* (Home Office Advisory Council on Child Care 1970). The guide made no mention of the desirability of 'same-race' adoption or the need to recruit black families. Court judgements which supported white private foster carers in disputes with Nigerian parents also appeared to endorse the desirability of transracial placements (CRC 1975: 35).

Transracial adoption in context

Having looked at the emergence of transracial adoption, it is now time to return to its wider social and political context. The 1960s saw major changes in both adoption and the politics of 'race' in Britain. Adoptions peaked in 1968 at almost 25,000 or roughly 2 per cent of live births, driven up by the same social forces which would subsequently bring about their decline. Initially, the changing pattern of sexual mores which led to increased illegitimate births, including those of mixed parentage, was reflected directly in a greater number of children given up for adoption. By the late 1960s, however, the declining stigma of illegitimacy, allied to more freely available contraception and the legalization of abortion, began to reverse the trend and by 1977 the number of adoptions had returned to its 1950s level at around 12,000 per year, continuing to fall thereafter. In the absence of reliable figures, it is not possible to gauge accurately the impact of these changes upon the adoption of black and minority ethnic children, their number or the ethnic backgrounds of their adopters. What is rarely disputed, however, is that the decline in adoption was most marked in relation to 'healthy white babies', whose supply fell far short of matching demand. Henceforth, adoption would become increasingly focused on those regarded as 'hard-to-place', a category still taken to include 'coloured' children well into the 1970s (ABAA 1975: 2). It is not clear how many white adopters turned to transracial adoption as a result of such 'market forces', although it seems certain that a significant number did so, as was the case for TRA in the United States (Simon and Altstein 1977: 27; Small 1986: 83).

The 1960s were also to witness profound changes in the politics of 'race' and ethnicity in Britain (Saggar 1992: 67). From immigration control to the legal machinery of 'race relations' or policy on social disadvantage, developments during the decade gave rise to an enduring legacy. The nature of both the emergent political mainstream and the bases of its opposition were also later to exert a major influence upon adoption practice for minority ethnic children. It is for this reason that a brief excursus, to provide an overview of the period, is appropriate at this point. During the 1950s, the British government had attempted to manage the contradiction between universalist principles and racialized exclusion by publicly setting its face against immigration control (increasingly called for by some backbench MPs), while covertly attempting to institute controls (Holmes 1991: 55; Solomos 1993: 56–7). Racist violence in Notting Hill and Nottingham during 1958 acted as a catalyst for the abandonment of so-called 'laissez-faire' immigration policy. Although widely condemned, the attacks were quickly cast as 'understandable', an almost inevitable response to 'the colour problem'. The conceptual racializing of immigration hardened to the point where 'all immigrants were black and all blacks were immigrants' (Moore 1975: 23; Miles and Phizacklea 1984: 21). Growing clamour for immigration control led to the Commonwealth Immigrants Act of 1962, with its voucher system based on labour market requirements being used to squeeze out black immigration steadily over the next decade (Solomos 1993: 64). From an initial position of principled opposition, the Labour Party was rapidly converted to the need for controls, notably after the electors of Smethwick made plain the strength of white working class views (Anwar 1986: 18–19). The new Labour government dropped plans to repeal the 1962 Act, actually strengthened its restrictions, and notoriously went on to introduce a further Commonwealth Immigrants Act in 1968. The latter represented a crude device to prevent Kenyan Asians with British passports entering Britain, by linking right of entry to having a parent or grandparent born in the United Kingdom. Subsequently termed 'patriality' under the Conservatives' 1971 Immigration Act, this principle should have destroyed any ideas that immigration was an issue of numbers rather than colour. Following the Act, the 'bad news' was that many more people were able to enter Britain. The 'good news' was that they were, almost without exception, white. Children adopted from abroad were classified as patrials.

Doubtless concerned to deflect allegations of racism in its immigration policy, the Labour Party evolved its 'dual strategy' (Solomos 1993: 83), coupling immigration controls with legislation against racial discrimination and the establishment of bodies to promote 'good race relations'. Combined, such measures were aimed at integration, an ill-defined term which moved rapidly from the vague to the virtually meaningless (Deakin 1970: 22). Whatever its meaning, the Labour government was clear that it fitted hand-in-glove with immigration control. In Roy Hattersley's famous formulation, 'integration without control is impossible, but control without integration is indefensible' (cited in Deakin 1970: 106). Responding to mounting evidence of 'colour bars' and pressure from the newly formed Campaign Against Racial Discrimination (CARD), the Labour government introduced the 1965 Race Relations Act, which took the first timid steps towards outlawing racial discrimination. Initially this applied only to public places, such as social and leisure facilities, but in 1968 was extended to employment and housing after research evidence showed massive discrimination in these areas (Daniel 1968). Daniel's findings (from a study undertaken by research group Political and Economic Planning (PEP)) were also powerful in their explosion of the notion that discrimination was based on 'newness' (perhaps no surprise to the black populations of Liverpool or Cardiff; Deakin 1970: 312) or lack of educational qualifications. Such rationalizations were wearing ever thinner. Evidence of pervasive discrimination also called into question the optimistic findings of an influential, but contentious, survey into prejudice which concluded that only 10 per cent of the native population were seriously prejudiced (Rose *et al.* 1969).[2]

However neat Roy Hattersley's phraseology, the coupling of immigration control and race relations is revealing of the politics of 'race' in Britain in a deeper sense. Critics have readily pointed to the paradox whereby in order to eliminate racial discrimination in Britain it had to be practised at the borders or, as Small puts it, a case of 'love thy neighbour, who shouldn't be here in the first place' (1994: 62). Moreover, a powerful message was sent by the contrast between strong, often over-zealous, enforcement of immigration controls and weak policing of anti-discrimination laws (Jones 1977: 162).

The middle years of the 1960s heralded a significant change in policy direction, witnessing the demise of 'naive assimilationism' and new initiatives to deal, albeit obliquely, with 'racial disadvantage'. In practice, assimilation involved an amalgam of aspiration and social engineering, notably in so-called 'dispersal' policies. Perhaps the best known of the latter was the early 1960s rule which limited the number of 'immigrant' children in any school to 30 per cent (Deakin 1970: 171), but dispersal was also practised by housing authorities, employers and even children's homes (Patterson 1965: 238). Retreat from naive assimilation was prompted by several factors. These included its manifest failure to reduce discrimination and the predictable side effects of crude social engineering. Above all, it became apparent that assimilation was not going to take place. On the one hand, significant sections of white society were clearly unwilling to accord equal status, regardless of how 'British' or 'English' black migrants or settlers became. On the other, and at least partly as a response to such exclusion, the latter actively resisted assimilation. For those from the Caribbean, Hiro (1973) gives an account of the gradual emergence of a 'West Indian' identity (p. 44) and the steady growth in separate provision, whether religious or social, and self-help in areas such as housing. Hiro notes (1973: 84) that for the second generation 'voluntary separatism . . . had become an accepted norm'. For most Asian groups, whose economic motivation for migration was often clearer, and whose culture was in some senses more sharply differentiated from that of white Britain, wholesale assimilation was even less appealing. Mirroring developments in the United States (Glazer and Moynihan 1970), society as 'melting pot' gave way, in principle, to that of 'cultural pluralism'.

and cultural heritage for survival in a racist society, bore the hallmarks of militant black struggles and of black nationalist influences in particular (Simon and Altstein 1977: 50). The significant time lag before such ideas would become powerful in Britain was predictable for two main reasons. The first is that in the early 1970s there were few black social workers and no obvious base inside or outside social work around which they could organize. (By contrast, mobilizations on educational issues were much more developed in the late 1960s and 1970s; Gabriel 1994: 81; Brah 1996: 40.) The second is that reliance on same-race adoption seemed much more of a possibility in the United States at that time. Even at the peak time for TRA in the US in 1971, it only accounted for roughly one-third of adoptions of black children (Simon and Altstein 1977: 30; Day 1979: 93). Despite the lack of accurate figures in Britain, it is safe to assume that the proportion of white families involved was significantly higher than in the US during the 1970s (ADSS/CRE 1978: 24). Research studies suggest that, even in the early 1980s, over 80 per cent of minority ethnic adoptions in the UK were transracial (Hill *et al.* 1989; Charles *et al.* 1992).

While a concerted attack on TRA was still some way off, there was nonetheless a growing expression of the concerns which would later fuel it. Discussion of these will form the basis of later chapters, but it is useful at this point to chart their historical emergence. Questions of identity for adoptees had taken on an increasing importance since the 1950s (Haimes and Timms 1985: 14). Initially, this was understood in terms of personal identity and revolved around the rights of adopted people to know of their adoption and the background leading to it, and the possibility of their being able to trace birth relatives if they so wished. These moves away from the 'clean break' view of adoption took place both informally, with the importance stressed of letting children know of their adoption, and formally through the 1975 Children Act which allowed adoptees access to their original birth certificate and the potential to commence tracing. They reflected a growing view that interest in birth family was both natural and psychologically healthy (Haimes and Timms 1985: 50). Cohen observes how identity came to be viewed in terms of a birthright or inheritance and how for black children this was racialized and collectivized, with black identity entailing 'actively locating an individual life history within the collective memory of a "race"' (1994: 59). As noted earlier, themes of racial and cultural identity were central to black struggles in the 1960s, and these began to filter through to the worlds of adoption and social work from that time on. The demise of assimilationism was noted, along with the rise of new and more militant black identities among second generation migrants (John 1972; Triseliotis 1972). Cheetham writes of social workers being seen as establishment lackeys and proffers the gloomy verdict that 'the social workers who can make useful relationships with this new generation of coloured people will be exceptional' (1972: 77).

Culture was seen as an important part of identity, closely linked to personality formation and providing a secure base from which to deal with difficulties (Kent 1972: 39; Triseliotis 1972a: 2). In this context, black and minority ethnic children in foster care or adopted were seen as vulnerable. Pryce talks of the threat posed to black children's cultural identity in white homes, the danger of internalizing negative images and resultant 'disturbing psychological problems' (CRC 1975: 7, 23–4). Living in white areas and Anglicization were seen as likely to alienate black children from family, culture and community, rendering them racially black but culturally white, and making future relations more difficult (Triseliotis 1972: 12; CRC 1975: 24). Where once the feasibility of TRA had been questioned due to largely implicit assumptions about racial divisions, its desirability was now challenged on the basis of much more explicit accounts of those divisions. Growing black assertiveness meant that the criteria by which substitute family care for black children was to be judged would become more demanding, and the ability of white families to measure up increasingly challenged. Introducing her follow-up study of the British Adoption Project, Jackson notes the more critical climate surrounding TRA. 'There is a developing feeling, particularly among black social workers, that the disadvantages to the child's cultural and racial identity outweigh all the other advantages. The question undoubtedly arises, are we creating essentially white children in brown and black bodies?' (1976: 5).

Informally, the pressure was increased by many birth mothers, particularly African–Caribbean, expressing a clear choice that their children should be placed with a black adoptive family (Independent Adoption Society 1975; Gaber 1994: 18). Arguably the most important development in the 1970s, however, was the challenge to recruitment practices. As has been noted, the desirability in principle of same-race adoption had rarely been disputed. Rather, the necessity for TRA was seen to rest on the shortfall of black families able or willing to adopt. With the mounting challenge to TRA, shortfall became, and remains, one of the main planks in its defence (Aldridge 1994). The Soul Kids Campaign launched in 1975 represented the first concerted effort at recruiting black adoptive families for children. While its success was limited if judged in the number of eventual adopters, it had more powerful effects in its critique of existing practice. The debate on recruitment will be considered further in Chapter 5, but the critique can usefully be summarized at this point. In essence, it was argued that adoption agencies had evolved their practice around an assumption of adoption as a white middle class phenomenon. This was reflected in everything from advertising to assessment and judgements about the nature of family and the suitability of adopters (Day 1979). The shortfall of black adoptive families began to be seen as the result of such 'Eurocentrism' rather than material circumstances or lack of a cultural tradition of formal adoption. In due course (see below), the gauntlet would be thrown down to adoption agencies – and the recruitment of black families seen as a measure of their commitment and competence.

This critique of adoption (and fostering) practice should be seen in the wider context of developments in social work, where 'race' and ethnicity were beginning to force their way onto organizational agendas. One indicator of growing significance can be detected within the literature on radical social work, by comparison between earlier and later works: a colour-blind class analysis (Bailey and Brake 1975; Corrigan and Leonard 1978) giving way to recognition of the specificity of 'race' issues (Husband 1980). In more established circles, the report of the ADSS/CRE (1978) working party (set up to examine local authority duties following the 1976 Race Relations Act) can also be seen as evidence of climate change, albeit mild, in Social Services Departments (SSDs). Notwithstanding its title, *Multi-racial Britain*, or the passage of much water under the bridge of immigration, it was still within the framework of newness, adjustment and resentment from the host community that the working party chose to locate its analysis. Also reported were the results of a revealing survey which found the SSDs' response to multi-racial Britain 'confused and ad hoc' (p. 7), with very little ethnic monitoring, use of s11 funding (see also Young 1983: 294) or effort to recruit minority ethnic social workers. The report's conclusion that 'services should recognise the new dimension of colour as important and not deny its existence' probably gives an accurate indication of contemporary social work practice and thinking on 'race' and ethnicity. In doing so, it helps to explain why opposition to TRA still remained marginal in the late 1970s.

If in some senses the 1970s saw less seismic shifts in the wider politics of 'race' and ethnicity than the 1960s, there were nonetheless developments which would be of importance for policy and practice in adoption. To paraphrase soccer parlance, the 1970s can be seen as 'a decade of two halves', with the economic crisis of 1975–6 prompting reaction and political realignments. The role of economic crisis was largely catalytic, though highly significant in determining those ideas 'whose time had come . . . and gone'. The ideas themselves have longer histories. For the politics of 'race', Saggar characterizes the whole period from 1958 to 1976 as one of 'pragmatism' (1992: 102). During the early 1970s, the leaders of both major political parties held to the 'consensus' established in the 1960s, based on tight immigration control, good race relations and eschewing use of 'the race card'. The consensus was always a fragile one, squeezed between Powellism and fascism on the one hand and campaigns for racial justice and black militancy on the other. During the early 1970s, the political right increasingly mobilized to halt and roll back the gains of liberation struggles. 'Race' played a key part in their picture of crumbling social order – whether in the racialized image of the young black 'mugger', or the implicitly causal association with inner-city decay (Hall *et al.* 1978). More broadly, the liberal interventionist state was blamed for the breakdown, having foisted immigration upon the white population and then failed to deal strongly enough with its consequences. In what Miles and Phizacklea (1984: 96) term its liberal phase from 1974 to 1976, the Labour government appeared to give greater weight to its race relations policy, with a mild easing of immigration controls and the strengthening of anti-discrimination law through the 1976 Race Relations Act. Thereafter, as immigration once again became more politicized, controls were tightened, including the infamous virginity tests and the X-raying of children (Gordon 1983; Brah 1996: 39).

This politicization was due both to changes within the Conservative Party and the influence of the National Front. The replacement of Ted Heath by Margaret Thatcher as Tory leader signalled a major change of direction towards a more populist approach to politics, including that of 'race' and ethnicity (Saggar 1992: 117). Drawing on Powellite themes, Thatcher spoke of the white population's legitimate fears of being 'swamped' by those of an alien culture, and of its fairness and tolerance being overstrained (Barker 1981: 13). By appealing to the great achievements of the British Empire, immigration served as a clear marker of decline (Saggar 1992: 120). She promised an end to all immigration, including that of dependants, and a weakening of 'race relations' law (Sivanandan 1982: 43). Almost equally important was the role of the National Front during the 1970s, not only in its direct activities but its raising the spectre of an upsurge in racist, fascist violence. In electoral terms the Front's support grew sharply from 1972 – following the arrival in Britain of expelled Ugandan Asians – and peaked in 1976–7 (Miles and Phizacklea 1984: 122; Anwar 1986: 139). More significant, however, was its complementary relationship with 'respectable' racism. On the one hand, as Saggar suggests, the National Front acted as a 'catalyst for greater elite responsiveness to grass-roots anti-black, anti-immigrant sentiment' (1992: 182). On the other, such responsiveness appeared to offer at least tacit support for the Front's growing violence. By 1979, however, its electoral support had collapsed (though not its involvement in violence), the result in part of the successful campaign of the Anti-Nazi League, but also because the Conservative Party had, to a significant extent, stolen its clothes.

Countering such forces, black resistance and struggles for racial equality continued on a number of fronts, from the workplace to the education system, while racist violence was increasingly confronted on the streets (Sivanandan 1982). The second PEP (Smith 1977) study showed little sign of declining discrimination, providing ever clearer evidence that its extent had little to do with the 'newness' of immigration. In this context, it is hardly surprising that the second generation had become, by common consent, 'less willing to compromise in the face of discrimination and racism' (Benson 1981: viii).

The significance of such developments for adoption operated at different levels. To a greater or lesser extent, and largely unchronicled, the politics of 'race' and ethnicity would have impacted on the lives of those individuals and families directly involved. In the wider domains of policy, the principal effect was the increasingly polarized political environment which had come to prevail. In the following decade, polarization would continue, with the issues of identity and culture central to the struggle.

The rise of 'same race' policies in the 1980s

For 'race', ethnicity and adoption, the 1980s was to be a decade of radical transformation, bringing significant upheavals within the relatively closed world of adoption, but also periodic controversies which entered into the wider public domain. The transformation reflected both 'internal' changes – in adoption, child care and social work – and the 'external', stemming from the new political landscape of Thatcher's Britain.

As the literature of the early 1980s reveals, analysis of the place of 'race' and ethnicity within social work was expanding rapidly in breadth and depth (Cheetham *et al.* 1981; Cheetham 1982). Questions ranging from race policies and ethnic monitoring in local authorities, the treatment of black elders, working across cultures, relations with minority ethnic communities, and training for staff, to the place of black workers in 'white' organizations, all came under closer scrutiny. Both the analysis and the initiatives described give a clear sense of the growing importance of 'race' issues, and of the black presence within social work. Needless to say, prominence was given in such work to child care (Ahmed 1981; James 1981) and specifically to adoption and fostering for black children (ABAFA 1981; Arnold 1982; Bagley and Young 1982). Local studies published at the same time showed continuing over-representation of black children in the care system, suggesting an urgent need for more preventive work (Adams 1981; Wilkinson 1982). As to family placement for those in the system, there were signs that, in multiracial areas at least, the need to recruit more black families was at last receiving serious recognition within SSDs (Draper 1981: 25). More broadly, there were also signs of a same-race philosophy gaining ground within social work (Fitzgerald 1981).

The work of the New Black Families Unit, established jointly by the Independent Adoption Service and Lambeth SSD in 1980, was to prove a major influence. Building on the critique of traditional recruitment methods, the unit sought to implement a more ethnic-sensitive approach, less rigid in terms of criteria for adoptive families and with less emphasis on formality (Arnold 1982; Small 1982). Its relative success fuelled the belief that the shortage of black families was primarily the result of agency failure or even 'institutional racism'. Thus armed, campaigners for same-race placements launched a scathing attack on transracial adoption, spearheaded by the newly formed Association of Black Social Workers and Allied Professionals (ABSWAP). In its evidence to the House of Commons Select Committee, ABSWAP described TRA as 'a microcosm of the oppression of black people in this society', a form of one-way traffic, depriving black communities of their most valuable resources. 'It is in essence, "internal colonialism" and a new form of slave trade, but this time only black children are used' (ABSWAP 1983).

By coincidence, in the same year, 1983, Gill and Jackson's follow-up of the British Adoption Project was published. Understandably in the new climate of race politics, their verdict that the adoptions were generally very successful, while noting that the children had become 'white in all but skin colour', did little to soothe passions. To the critics of TRA, the findings seemed to provide clear evidence of its failings in relation to racial and cultural identity (Divine 1983; Small 1986). In the mid-1980s, radical London boroughs began to evolve policies in support of same-race adoption and fostering which opponents claimed amounted to a 'prohibition' on transracial placements. Thus were the new battle lines drawn, with same-race policies seen alternatively as a prerequisite for commitment to fighting racism or as political dogma which flew in the face of research evidence. The pressure group Children First in Transracial Fostering and Adoption was formed in 1986 to expose and oppose what it cast as the rigidities of same-race policies. The first major press and television debates were held, notably between two black social workers, Ben Brown and David Divine, defending and opposing TRA respectively.

If this new situation was to a degree generated from within social work, it also owed a good deal to wider political struggles. The terrain was varied, from institutional questions such as central–local government relations or separate organization for minority groups, through to ideological disputes over the causes of racial inequality or the (racial) identity of Britain. The electoral victories of Margaret Thatcher and Ronald Reagan had brought the 'new right' to government in Britain and the United States, exerting a major influence on both economic and social policies. The ideological project of the new right was to roll back the gains of the Great Transformation and dismantle the liberal interventionist state which it had helped to spawn. Though the project was by no means solely or even primarily a racial one, it had a strong 'racial sub-text'. As Omi and Winant argue, in a world of democratic and universal values, and with liberation struggles still relatively fresh in the memory, there could be no disavowal of the principle of racial equality (1994: 117). Rather, the new right strategy was to redefine equality in line with the 'natural order' which they sought to restore – based on competitive individualism in a free market, with greater reliance on self and family and less on the (welfare) state. Above all, equal opportunity entailed the right to be unequal within this natural order. Theoretically colour blind in conception and aim, the ensuing policies were generally refracted through a racialized social order; to the detriment of minority communities, albeit unevenly in terms of class, gender and ethnicity. As Small wryly observes, while recent decades have seen increasing black stratification, there remain 'more paupers than princes, mendicants than millionaires' (1994: 111).

The new right's project had little place for anything beyond the most basic of anti-discrimination measures, and was scornful of attempts to 'engineer equality'. In the United States, this meant increasing attacks on affirmative action programmes (depicted as discriminating against white people) and the civil rights 'industry' (Omi and Winant 1994: 80; Marable 1995: 81). By implication the quest for racial equality had gone too far. In Britain, it had travelled less far, but definitely far enough for the new right.

Lacking easy targets such as affirmative action, the campaign was waged more at an ideological level. A broadly twin-track approach mixed official (i.e. government) denial of any real problem of racial discrimination with unofficial (maverick MPs, media pundits and new right theorists) baiting and ridiculing of anyone who made such claims. Also targetted were those – in Britain notably the trade unions and welfare professionals – whose values and links with the liberal state made them antipathetic to the radical right. While neither anti-discrimination laws nor unions and professionals had a glowing record in combating racism, their relative disempowerment did have the effect of weakening bases from which such struggles could be waged (Gordon 1990).

The new right's cultural agenda in Britain focused on the (re)creation of a sense of bounded community and the reinvigoration of British nationalism (Barker 1981: 21; Mason 1995: 115). It was unashamedly assimilationist in tenor, opposed to 'multiculturalism' or the notion of a 'multiracial' society (Saggar 1992: 178; Solomos 1993: 107). The virtues of colour blindness were counterposed to the divisiveness of racial identities. As the 1983 Conservative election poster, showing a smartly dressed black man, proclaimed, 'Labour says he's Black, Tories say he's British'. (Clearly swayed, over 80 per cent of African–Caribbeans voted Labour.) The emphasis on (white) British culture allied to sociobiological ideas of a 'natural preference for one's own kind' led some to talk of a 'new racism' (Barker 1981) although, as Small comments, many older variants of racism also still persisted (1994: 12).

Amid the political and ideological ascendancy of new right influences, local government became an important battleground. The early 1980s split in the Labour Party was reflected in certain authorities in London (including the GLC) and other major cities coming under control of the 'new urban left' which prioritized equal opportunities issues and saw its role as defending local people against the ravages of Thatcherism (King 1989: 201). Particularly in London authorities, black representation was growing significantly, giving further impetus to anti-racist struggles (Butcher et al. 1990: 121). The urgency of tackling racism was also fuelled by the aftermath of the urban disorders of 1981, with Lord Scarman (1982) identifying social deprivation as a factor alongside poor and deteriorating relationships between black communities and the police. The third PEP (now Policy Studies Institute) study also confirmed the continuing prevalence of discrimination, with black people facing higher levels of unemployment, underemployment relative to skills and qualifications and poorer housing (Brown 1984).

The new approach to (race) equality had three major characteristics. The first was to apply an analysis which emphasized power and institutional discrimination, and demanded institutional strategies rather than simply 'education'. These included development of specific policies and monitoring, but also the organizational presence of equality committees and/or units (Small 1994: 166–7). A second related feature was the principle of separate organization, the logic of which was that those facing discrimination or oppression needed space to discuss relevant issues and experiences, and a base from which to challenge the wider institution. In the 1980s, Black workers' groups would become a customary feature of such authorities and those which followed their lead. This principle was also strong in the early to mid-1980s in many trade unions and the campaign for Black sections in the Labour Party (Saggar 1992: 133; Solomos 1993: 208), and implicit in the sharp rise of 'black-led' organizations (Sivanandan 1982: 40–1). The third key characteristic was the use of 'Black' as an inclusive term for all those facing racism, in some instances even extending to clearly 'white' Jewish and Irish people. Within this formulation, ethnicity took a subordinate role and was, in any strong expression, seen as divisive to anti-racist struggle.

If, as we shall see, all three of these elements would come under pressure from those sympathetic to the cause, the major assault came from more predictable quarters. In popular ideology, 'the loony left' became the catchphrase for attacks on the new urban left and particularly their equality policies, which were alternately ridiculous ('Baa Baa Green Sheep') and sinister ('the thought police'). The Conservative government strategy ranged from the financial constraints of the Poll Tax and capping, through limiting, bypassing and removing powers of local authorities, to outright abolition in the case of the GLC, the Metropolitan Counties and, later, the Inner London Education Authority (ILEA).

As to the impact of local anti-racist struggles, it must be remembered that local authorities varied and continue to vary widely in their priorities. In their study of equal opportunities policies, Young and Connelly (1981) produced a fourfold typology of local authorities – pioneers, learners, waverers, and resisters. There is little doubt that some social work agencies made significant gains in the recruitment and promotion of black social workers, including some high-profile appointments at directorate level.[3] Yet developments were patchy. A CRE Survey (1989) found Social Services Departments taking 'race' issues more seriously than in 1979, but only a minority having equal opportunities policies or monitoring arrangements. The overall verdict of Butcher *et al.* at the end of the 1980s is unflattering, describing local government as 'an institution rotten with racism and sexism', its anti-racist, race equality and multicultural programmes 'largely marginal, symbolic and cosmetic' (1990: 134).

Disillusionment with the relative lack of progress achieved by 'municipal anti-racism' combined with wider forces to weaken its main tenets. There was increasing recognition that institutional measures were limited without a successful battle for hearts and minds. Critics such as Paul Gilroy attacked the 'statist' approach to anti-racism and the effects of class division within black communities, positing a 'conspicuous divergence of interests between the never-employed and the cadre of black bureaucrats employed by the local state to salve their misery' (cited in Small 1994: 137). The Black umbrella also came under scrutiny, some wishing to emphasize its permeability as opposed to 'essentialist' views of identity and culture (see Chapter 4), while others at least partially forsook its shelter by reclaiming Asian identities from the African–Caribbean hegemony of 'Black' (Modood 1992). The re-emergence of ethnicity was further underlined in the late 1980s by the controversy surrounding Salman Rushdie's *Satanic Verses*, which highlighted the salience of religion, notably in the identity of British Muslims (Gabriel 1994: 22–9). A research study by Yawar (1992) showed that relatively little attention was being paid by most child care agencies to the needs of Muslim children.

Summarizing the significance of such developments for adoption (and fostering) in the 1980s, it can be seen that the mounting challenge to trans-racial adoption found fertile ground in the local politics of many multi-racial areas. While same race policies found a natural home in left Labour authorities, their currency ran much wider, influencing Conservative as well as more traditional Labour authorities. A CRE survey of social services departments found fostering and adoption policies figuring prominently among 'race initiatives', roughly 25 per cent having written policies (1989: 20), while Butt *et al.* (1991) found that 63 per cent of local authorities in multi-racial areas had same-race policies. Same-race policies and their attendant rationale were also increasingly supported by major child care organizations such as Barnardos, National Children's Homes, and both British Agencies for Adoption and Fostering (BAAF) and National Foster Care Association (NFCA).

One reason for this spread beyond the confines of new urban left authorities was that 'anti-racism' was a developing theme within social work itself (Dominelli 1988). Among various social work initiatives was the establishment of the Race Equality Unit in 1987 and a Black Perspectives Committee at the Central Council for Education and Training in Social Work (CCETSW) in the same year. 'Anti-racist' (along with the broader anti-discriminatory) practice became a key feature of the competency require-ments for the Diploma in Social Work launched in 1989.

If, on the one hand, such developments indicate a sea change in social work and child care practice, it is also important to remember their uneven-ness – between and within agencies and localities, management and social work teams. In Young and Connelly's (1981) terms there would be both pioneers and resisters, and those in between. Barn (1993b) has noted how the research summarized as *Social Work Decisions in Child Care* (DHSS 1985) makes barely any mention of race issues. Rhodes (1992) provides a fascinating account of the complexities surrounding implementation of a same-race policy within one 'pioneering' London authority and of the wide variety of practice elsewhere in the capital. Outside the professional arena, Bagley's (1993) surveys of African–Caribbean views on 'race' and adoption provide interesting evidence of the changes taking place during the 1980s. Comparison of a 1979 survey and 1989 follow-up showed that while there was still 'general support' for transracial adoption, this had fallen sharply during the 1980s (1993: 256–63), a change Bagley rather glibly attributes to the policy-led decline in TRA.

The 1989 Children Act and the Major years

In relation to race, ethnicity and adoption, the 1989 Children Act can be seen as marking something of a watershed, from which there was to be gradual retreat during the 1990s. The Act gave the first formal recognition to issues of 'race' and ethnicity in statute child care law, requiring local authorities to give due consideration, in decision making for children 'looked after' by them, to 'religious persuasion, racial origin, and cultural and linguistic background' (s22(5)(c)). A late addition to the Act, prompted by a case in Croydon (see below), was the requirement that in efforts to recruit foster carers, local authorities should 'have regard to the different racial groups to which children within their area who are in need belong' (Schedule 2(11)(b)). Accompanying official guidance stated that 'since discrimination of all kinds is an everyday reality in many children's lives, every effort must be made to ensure that agency services and practices do not reflect or reinforce it' (cited in Freeman 1992: 74). Though advocates of same-race adoption and fostering were often to take the Children Act provisions as legal support for such policies, guidance was always more guarded and, as Allen (1990: 61) suggests, giving 'due consideration' is open to wide-ranging interpretation.

Part of the context for the Children Act's provisions was research evidence of continuing over-representation of black children, and particularly those of mixed parentage, in the care system (Bebbington and Miles 1989; Rowe *et al.* 1989). They were also influenced by the storm which broke in August 1989 when Croydon SSD removed a child of mixed parentage from a white foster family to place him with a black family for adoption. Media and political comment was overwhelmingly hostile to the social workers' actions and the court judgement which supported them (Johnson 1991; Kirton 1992). In addition to the legal change on recruitment noted above, the controversy also led to new guidance being issued (SSI 1990), which combined general support for the principle of matching placements with warnings against their rigid implementation. The media pot was kept boiling by other publicized removals of children from white foster homes, notably in Liverpool (The *Times*, 17 March 1990) and later Avon (*Community Care*, 17–23 September 1992).

The Children Act made only relatively minor changes to adoption law (still governed by the 1976 Adoption Act), but as part of its rolling programme of family law review, the government established a review in July 1989. This was seen as necessary for three main reasons. The first was to harmonize provisions with the Children Act, notably the emphasis on parental responsibilities and partnership, but also its provisions on race, religion, culture and language. A second was to consider fully the wide-ranging changes in adoption which had occurred since 1976, including growing advocacy for 'openness'. A third was to deal with inter-country adoption (ICA) in the light of the Hague Conference and its impending Convention. In the early 1990s, ICA took on a higher public profile as a result of developments in Romania and later Bosnia. Inevitably both the significant number of adoptions and the tactics involved rekindled debates about whether ICA in such circumstances is primarily humanitarian or opportunistic, child rescue or child snatching? After various background papers, the Inter-departmental Working Group issued a Green Paper in 1992 (DoH 1992). It had relatively little to say on issues of 'race' and ethnicity, beyond the need for continuing efforts to recruit minority ethnic adopters (p. 51). Thoburn, in her summary of research, reports that studies of transracial adoption have not borne out the fears of black social workers, but cites other research which suggests that such a positive picture may need to be viewed with caution (DoH 1992: 148–9). In relation to inter-country adoption, the review also (somewhat wishfully) supported the principle of ethnic matching while noting that a family of different racial origin or religion 'may be the best available choice' (p. 102).

The stance on 'race', ethnicity and adoption varied little from that at the time of the Children Act. However, as the review progressed towards legislation, it became steadily more influenced by the furore over 'political correctness' (PC) which had entered the political lexicon in the early 1990s. Fire was soon directed at social work in general, adoption and fostering practice in particular. Common sense became the watchword as the government took up cudgels against the 'anti-discriminatory' thrust of single parent, lesbian and gay, and same-race adoptions. There was a marked shift between the Green Paper and the White Paper, *Adoption: The Next Step*', published in November 1993 and widely taken to reflect the government's desire to promote 'family values'. As the political shadow cast by the 'underclass' debate lengthened, (young) single mothers were increasingly cast as both an economic burden and a symbol of moral decline. To right-wing think tanks such as the Institute of Economic Affairs, and commentators such as Patricia Morgan and Melanie Phillips, adoption was an 'obvious solution' (*Daily Telegraph*, 8 March 1995; *The Times*, 27 December 1996). The White Paper implicitly expressed concerns about the effect of the Children Act's emphasis on partnership with parents in giving them too much power and thereby leading to 'drift'. The other implicit concern was that social workers were, in their treatment of prospective adopters, placing unnecessary barriers in the way of the adoption process. A later circular (SSI 1996a) talked of social workers interrogating and humiliating adopters, subjecting them to their personal views and foisting inappropriate training upon them. PC was the unspoken thread running through much of this criticism. So marked was the shift of emphasis and so strident the tone of censure that many feared a return to the days when adoption was seen primarily as a service to childless parents.

Predictably, same-race adoption was seen as one of the unnecessary barriers to adoption and targetted accordingly. The hardening of attitude was also widely attributed to the 'Norfolk case' with a couple, one of whom was black, being refused as adopters, allegedly on the grounds of their 'naivety' about racism (*The Times*, 9 July 1993). As is frequently the case, the subsequent enquiry supported the decision, but interest in the facts had long since been crushed under the anti-PC juggernaut. The White Paper acknowledged the importance of ethnicity, but argued that it was often given 'unjustifiably decisive influence' (para 4.32). Nonetheless, the government indicated an intention to introduce a broad requirement on ethnicity and matching 'in line with what is now in the Children Act' (para 4.32).

However, momentum was gathering in the crusade against PC, and the Adoption Bill of 1996 omitted any reference to race. Enacted, this would have created the bizarre situation of local authorities being obliged to consider 'racial origin and cultural background' in decision making under the Children Act, including plans for adoption, while facing no such requirement under adoption law itself. Alongside the bill, a letter was issued by the Social Services Inspectorate (SSI 1996a) which attempted the political conjuring trick of setting out a change in policy while simultaneously denying it. The letter opened by stating that the principles of 1990 continued to apply. Yet whereas this guidance had set out carefully the many advantages of ethnic matching before giving its warnings on over-emphasis, its 1996 successor was lukewarm on the former and nothing if not persistent on the latter. For same-race adoption, gone was any reference to 'the great majority of cases'; 'other things being equal' was now pointedly underlined; and 'is most likely' to best meet the child's needs had been diluted to 'may well be most likely'. Sensitive discussion about the competing needs of children had given way to blunt warnings against 'unrealistic hopes' of ethnic matching, while the expectations of transracial adopters in respect of cultural heritage had been noticeably scaled down.

The letter also criticized what it saw as local authority hostility towards inter-country adoption. The controversies of the early 1990s had highlighted the often fraught relationship between (prospective) inter-country adopters and adoption agencies. In turn, the issues were articulated with domestic concerns around the (racial) politics of adoption. ICA was often seen as the result of babies or young children not being available within Britain and, crucially for its supporters, white parents being prevented from adopting minority ethnic British children. Adoption agencies were, with some justification, seen as being at best cool and often hostile to ICA because of its customary transracial, transcultural nature. This was cast as 'ideological opposition' based on PC and readily taken up in the government crusade. The 1996 SSI letter had dropped the earlier reference to ethnic matching in ICA and went on the offensive over cultural knowledge. 'It would be quite wrong . . . for adoption agencies to refuse to process an adoption application on the grounds that the applicants cannot furnish strong personal links with the country of their choice' (para. 16).

By a neat irony, the government's small majority, and fear of repeating the infighting which had dogged the Family Law Bill, led to the shelving of the Adoption Bill. Nonetheless, its campaign against PC in adoption continued unabated until the 1997 general election. In December 1996, John Major floated the idea of transferring adoption from local authorities to

also offered a significant voice within debates, with very active involvement of (transracial) adopters in research and writing on 'race' and adoption (Gaber and Aldridge 1994).

How, then, do liberal values such as individualism, reason and tolerance provide a framework for understanding issues of 'race' and ethnicity in adoption? Individualism is evident in the self-contained study of adoptive identities within the confines of the family and a methodology which largely ignores both psychodynamics and social structure in its investigations. Liberal faith in the power of reason is manifested in two main ways: first, in its being enshrined in 'objective' enquiry and second, in the belief that the resulting conclusions should hold sway over the direction of policy and practice. For the supporters of TRA, the claim that 'the evidence supports it' is clearly one of their most powerful (Richards 1994: 84). Finally, there is the self-image of tolerance and openness, which is contrasted with the 'dogma' of opponents. In relation to the research process, this can be seen in terms of the readiness to take up the criticisms levelled at TRA and investigate them fully.

'The evidence'

In a recent review of research into transracial placements, Rushton and Minnis (1997) list ten major studies from the United States and three from the United Kingdom.[1] Though each of these studies has its own distinctive methodological features and approaches to questions of identity, there is also a great deal of common ground which justifies their location within a 'liberal paradigm'. Research methods encompass various tests, interviews and questionnaires carried out with adopted children and significant others, notably adoptive parents and sometimes teachers. For the children three approaches dominate: doll tests to indicate (self)identifications and preferences; psychological tests, of personality, adjustment and variations on the theme of self-esteem, self-image or self-concept; and interviews, examining orientations, experiences of racism and satisfaction with adoption. Parents have either been interviewed or invited to complete questionnaires, broadly concentrating on their perceptions of the 'success' of the adoption and/or of the child's development. In two cases, teachers have completed questionnaires regarding academic progress and behaviour in school. Most studies have employed some form of comparison with transracial adoption, most frequently either children adopted 'inracially' by black families, or white adoptees and white birth children in adoptive families (see Rushton and Minnis 1997: 150–1 for a useful summary).

The overall message which emerges from this body of research is that transracial adoption is broadly 'successful' and that the concerns expressed about adoptees' (racial) identities are unfounded. Although a somewhat variable picture is drawn of their racial identities, there is nonetheless consensus that identities are 'positive'. It will be argued here that in its methods, findings and interpretation, this research promotes an over-simplified view of experiences within transracial adoption. Further, it will be suggested that this process is not 'neutral' in its effects, but is likely to be biased towards more positive views. This is not, however, to embrace the 'nightmare' view of TRA sometimes propagated by opponents, which is also dangerously over-simplified. Neither is it to deny the successful elements for many adoptees, although here too superficiality in research means that little light is cast upon them.

In examining the liberal research paradigm, it is important to note certain historical factors. The first is that study of identity was dominated in the 1960s and 1970s by psychological theories, and strongly influenced by Erikson's (1963) conceptualization of developmental stages and associated tasks. However, most studies conformed to the requirements of a scientific psychology by attempting to render identity or its surrogates measurable. This had the twin effects of substituting static snapshot views for developmental processes (Breakwell 1992: 6) and depleting Erikson's already circumscribed view of the social (Slugoski and Ginsburg 1989). A second factor was that study of racial identity was inextricably linked to the racial politics of the United States and to the phenomenon of black 'self-hatred'. This problematic, best known through the doll tests initiated by Clarke and Clarke, focused on issues of racial identification and preference on the part of young children (see Milner 1983 for review). The key question was the extent to which black children would show their desire to be white, as aspiration or self-delusion. (Needless to say, white preferences remained overwhelmingly white!) This research was, it should be noted, strongly underpinned by liberal values and aimed to highlight the damage suffered by black Americans through segregation (Mama 1995: 51). The message, however, was conveyed within the decontextualized confines of scientific psychology which left no doubt that whatever their origins, black pathology and self-hatred were real and psychologically deeply rooted (Hauser 1971).

This psychologism, already part of the liberal paradigm for study of racial identity, was readily transferred to the study of TRA and ironically reinforced by the black radical challenge. In part this reflected the limited break from liberalism made by 'black psychology' in its early days, notably in terms of conceptualization and research methods (Robinson 1995). Equally important was the fact that the construction of identity put forward by opponents of TRA implied that identity problems experienced by transracial adoptees would be both severe and readily detectable.

Testing, testing – into the dolls' house

Two major US studies have utilized techniques based on doll tests in relation to the study of adoptive identities. Simon and Altstein's study of black, native American and Asian adoptees and their white siblings led to bold claims that TRA had a significant 'perhaps even . . . revolutionary' impact on racial identity (1977: 161). The claim derived from the finding that, unlike many of their counterparts raised in black families, black children in white families did not demonstrate a 'white preference'. According to Simon and Altstein, transracial adoptees 'do not acquire the ambivalence toward their own race found in all other studies' (p. 158). The accuracy and confidence of adoptees identifications, however, was distinctly at odds with parental views, which were found to be marked by great uncertainty. Seventy five per cent of parents thought their white children saw themselves as white, but only 32 per cent thought that their black children saw themselves as black (p. 101). A rather different message emerged from the research of Johnson *et al.* who undertook a longitudinal study of black children adopted in white and black homes respectively. They found that while the children placed in white homes expressed greater preferences for black dolls or figures at the age of 4, this had reversed by the age of 8 with children in black homes then showing the stronger black preferences (1987: 50).

Such inconsistencies are, however, perhaps only reflective of deeper problems in the use of doll studies. Apart from questions of the perceived accuracy and familiarity to the children of different coloured dolls, there are problems in analysis and interpretation. For instance, there is little or no exploration of meanings attached to colour/'race'. Moreover, as Katz (1996: 14) rightly comments, there is minimal contextualization; for example, in spite of strong evidence of the influence of parental attitudes on children, doll studies only rarely attempt to link the two (Johnson *et al.* 1987: 51). Thus, the multifaceted bases upon which identifications and preferences rest are simplified, and in the case of 'race' and adoption hitched to a crude white/black dichotomy. The difficulties are compounded by ready translation of preferences into measures of identity itself and the assumption that results from dolls can be easily transferred to people. Yet, research which has looked at children's expressed racial preferences in doll tests and actual relationships has not found a close link (Katz 1996: 15). Finally, there is the belief on the part of investigators that the findings have a certain psychological durability, a belief clearly not borne out by their rapid change within the space of a decade (Milner 1983).

Testing, testing – parity of self-esteem?

Psychological tests of 'self' have been pivotal to research into TRA, providing, for many researchers, the most compelling evidence of its 'success'. We will return below to the relationship between self-esteem and racial identity in adoption, but it is clear that the latter has consistently exerted a brooding presence over study of the former. This stems from the black nationalist-led attack on TRA, which claimed that adoptees would suffer from low self-esteem or otherwise hold negative self-concepts (Chestang 1972: 102; Chimezie 1975). It was this charge that researchers took on within their chosen framework of psychological testing and 'refuted'. In the United States, several studies have reported high levels of self-esteem among transracial adoptees and comparable levels with children adopted into black families (McRoy and Zurcher 1983: 118; Simon and Altstein 1987: 75). In Britain, Bagley and Young (1979) found very similar scores between black and white adoptees in white homes, while Gill and Jackson (1983: 83) found transracial adoptees to have no signs of low self-esteem.

Before setting out a critical view of these studies, it must be stated that the argument will not be that they are meaningless, but rather that they are significantly less meaningful than their adherents assume. What they do largely lay to rest is the spectre of deep pathology, of pervasive and widespread psychological damage inflicted upon transracial adoptees. For although psychological testing is a very blunt instrument, it seems inconceivable that its results could be quite so misleading. That said, the weaknesses of such tests and their results are substantial. For the most part, they rest on a reified view of the subject, as possessed of a 'self' which can be gauged and placed along scales from high to low, positive to negative, on the basis of responses to statements. The key assumption is that testing can cut through psychodynamic processes and 'presentation of self' to codify core subjectivity directly. Yet the statements used are extraordinarily abstract and vague. Typical examples used by Gill and Jackson (1983: 84) include, 'On the whole I am satisfied with myself'; 'Sometimes I think I am no good at all'; and, 'I have a number of good qualities', and must be judged by readers as to their ultimate usefulness. While some tests attempt to allow for problems such as 'defensive self-esteem', notably by including 'lie' questions which cast doubt on other responses (Bagley 1993: 200), they remain firmly trapped within the same empiricist framework. The tests are similarly neglectful of social structure. This is most obvious in the universalist approach to self or identity across social divisions of class, 'race' or gender. Terms such as 'well-adjusted' are taken to need no further exploration. Questions of self as 'who' or 'what', or as constructed from which sources of identification, are buried beneath the scaling exercises. In effect, the latter serve as proxies for a mental health, the universalist pretensions of which have long since been discredited (Penfold and Walker 1984; Fernando 1991; Ussher 1991; Nazroo 1997). It must be recognized that measures of self-esteem provide far too crude a device for tackling the complexities of adoptive identities (Ryburn 1994b: 27). It is noteworthy that while studies have shown no differences between adoptees and non-adoptees in terms of self-esteem, the former have had markedly higher clinical referral rates (Brodzinsky 1990; Hoopes 1990; Lau 1993: 165).

Squaring the circle? Self and racial identity

If opponents of TRA are thought to be sent reeling by the high levels of self-esteem enjoyed by transracial adoptees, the knock-out blow surely comes from an equally consistent finding, namely that these levels are not linked to racial identity. This in turn raises the question of whether racial identity 'matters', and in what ways. All studies acknowledge, both implicitly and explicitly, the major differences of upbringing in white and black adoptive families. The significance of this for the identities of black children, however, is interpreted in diverse ways, which can usefully be categorized within two approaches. The first, typified by Gill and Jackson, is a broadly assimilationist view, namely that while the children take on 'white identities', this does not act as an impediment and may even be advantageous in certain respects. The second, represented particularly in Simon and Altstein's longitudinal study, is that children develop black identities which are 'different but equal' in relation to more normative versions. We will return to discussion of these two interpretive schools, but first consider the reported findings and their bases.

As with treatment of self-esteem itself, closer scrutiny of research into its relationship with racial identity raises serious doubts about its value. In particular, the oft-repeated 'independence' of racial identity and self-esteem at least partly reflects methodological weaknesses and is arguably as much a presupposition of the research as a result of it. Many of the problems stem from the conceptualization of racial identity which is rooted firmly within an empiricist framework. It is assumed that racial identity can be gauged through a mix of self-identification labels, and markers such as patterns of friendship and expressed preferences in social geography. There is little attempt to explore either the intra-psychic aspects of identity or the wider social meanings and discourses linked to racialization. Thus, identities become implicitly self-generated.

The most developed version of the 'independence' thesis comes from Feigelman and Silverman (1983, 1984). Their research is based on multivariate analysis of 737 questionnaires completed by white American adopters of white, African–American, Korean and Colombian children respectively. Feigelman and Silverman found that racial identities were significantly influenced by parental socialization and ethnic composition of localities, but these factors were not found to be related to the adjustment of African–American (or Colombian) children. Observing that this contradicts the seemingly obvious link between racial pride and psychological functioning, the authors' conclusion is that 'a transracial adoptee can be well-adjusted and identified with the black community, white society or both' (1983: 119). Despite its impressive statistics, Feigelman and Silverman's analysis suffers from major weaknesses, the most important of which is the reliance on adopters for information which is used to gauge both adjustment and racial identity. To refract children's racial identities through the prism of (white) parental perceptions is surely to build on shaky foundations, creating difficulties which sophisticated statistical analysis is likely to compound rather than alleviate. It is scarcely reassuring to find them using a generalized category of 'discomfort with physical appearance' across racialized lines, implicitly equating the effects of colour racism with having spots or weight problems. The weaknesses of Feigelman and Silverman's approach are nowhere more evident than when they conclude, from comparison of their different groups of adoptees, that black Americans, but not Koreans, can be well-adjusted while suffering shame regarding their racial background.

In their British study, Gill and Jackson use a mixture of 'self-perception' and 'orientation' to gauge identities. Rightly mindful of the danger of assuming the dominance of 'race' or ethnicity in identity, they opt for a more inductive approach (1983: 13). 'Race' and ethnicity were rarely mentioned in response to prescribed questions such as 'a time when I was happy . . . or proud . . .', and on this basis, Gill and Jackson suggest that they did not have an 'overriding significance . . . in terms of how these children experience their lives' (p. 95). When statements were couched in more overtly racialized forms e.g. 'a time when I was proud to be black . . .', the most common response given was of 'not having to get a sun tan' (p. 96). Gill and Jackson go on to note the often negative views held of black communities and the lack of interest in them, or identification with them, on the part of adoptees. Friendships were overwhelmingly white, a finding common to most studies of TRA (McRoy and Zurcher 1983: 69; Simon *et al.* 1994: 96). Gill and Jackson do not directly compare racial identity with self-esteem scores for respondents, but rather cast the relationship at a more abstract level, i.e. that generally high self-esteem, combined with generally weak black identification, refutes the notion of any necessary, positive link between the two.

Gill and Jackson's approach provides an excellent example of research within the liberal paradigm and its parameters. While the intentions of their inductive approach are commendable, the result is a research study which tells us relatively little about the inner thoughts and feelings of adoptees on 'race' or the contexts within which they had developed. Like most other studies of adoption and 'race', there is minimal exploration of what terms of self-definition – brown, mixed, black (or white) etc. – signify to those who employ them. There is also a failure to acknowledge the sensitivities surrounding both adoption itself and its racial dynamics which mean that those interviewed are likely to be highly guarded in what they reveal to strangers. Aside from questions of love and family loyalty (Ladner 1977: 152; Simon and Altstein 1987: 105; Mullender 1988a: 132), there are those of trust in interviewers who will also be talking to parents.[2] If adoptees are unused to discussing 'race' issues within the family, they are highly unlikely to do so volubly with researchers. Moreover, even if so inclined, they may lack a ready vocabulary, bearing in mind that recognition and awareness are to an extent mutually reinforcing. Finally, there is the question of psychological threat. As one transracial adoptee starkly puts it, 'If I accept that same-race placements are the right ones then I have to say that my childhood is wiped away' (Mallows 1991: 90). Taken together, these factors are apt to lead to significant silences on the importance of 'race' and ethnicity in the lives of adoptees. Although this may lead to an under-reporting of positive aspects, including challenges successfully met, the major impact is likely to fall on difficulties experienced. Even where these do emerge, they may be glossed over by researchers. For instance, Jackson describes almost half the adoptees as 'anxious about race and colour' yet does not discuss this further (1976: 27), while Simon *et al.* acknowledge a racial aspect to adjustment, but offer no comment on what it might be (1994: 67). It is often narrative accounts which offer greater insights, as in Lesley's description of her son's anger and confusion over identity. 'He played heavy black rap music all the time, wore Public Enemy T-shirts and wept bitterly over a film about Steve Biko. But he determinedly avoided being in company with black people unless he knew them. When forced into discussion about racism or racial differences he would say that all people were the same under the skin and that it didn't matter to him' (1996: 162).

The nature of the relationship found between self-esteem and racial identity within this research tradition must therefore be understood partly through both terms being decontextualized and reified before being correlated. When self-esteem is constructed within a universalist, deracialized language, and racial identity gauged on an narrow individualistic basis, the likelihood of meaningful exploration is limited. The value of structured responses to statements such as 'I feel confused being a black child of mixed race in a white family' (Bagley 1993: 255) must surely be questioned as a means of teasing out the nuances, contingencies, and 'double consciousness' of black racialized experience (Gilroy 1993). Within this context, the 'independence' of self-esteem and racial identity is hardly surprising.

Whether reflective of such concerns or not, it is possible to detect within the research studies a degree of unease over the findings on self-esteem and racial identity. An undercurrent of ambivalence is not difficult to explain. For if a lack of relationship between the two seemingly obviates the need for a 'positive black identity', it raises the spectre of 'success' gained through 'honorary white' status. It must be remembered here that the liberal paradigm is neither avowedly assimilationist nor insensitive to issues of racial inequality. Though never stated explicitly, it is reasonable to suppose that researchers would have welcomed finding strong black identities among transracial adoptees.

Thus, Gill and Jackson, while offering a broadly assimilationist view, nonetheless seem to endorse the logic of same-race placements. On identity, for instance, they call for transracial adopters to make stronger links with black communities and strengthen the children's sense of racial identity and heritage (1983: 139). Gill and Jackson's ambivalence may stem from their findings on adoptees' 'denial' of racial background, with its negative psychological, ethical and political connotations. Bagley's (1993) position on transracial and inter-country adoption is also assimilationist in tenor. Pride of place is given to 'adjustment' which, in addition to adoptive family dynamics, also depends upon the level of discrimination faced by the minority ethnic group concerned. Assuming this is low enough to permit assimilation, then the latter is unproblematic for Bagley. Thus, while he is damning of the 'imperialistic' adoption of native peoples in North America (p. 237), he is sanguine about inter-country adoption in Britain. He comments favourably upon 'cheerful, Anglicized teenagers, full of self-confidence, dating freely with their English peers' (p. 162) and argues that for those adopted from Hong Kong 'it seems inevitable that the very process of absorption into an accepting family and culture will diminish both interest in and need for a clear ethnic identity which is different from that of the adopted culture' (p. 203). That Britain is an accepting culture will no doubt come as welcome, if somewhat surprising, news to many of Chinese origin (Parker 1995), but there is little doubt that Bagley glosses over the complexities and difficulties of racialization in his upbeat stance.[3] Perhaps his division between the 'imperialistic' and 'non-imperialistic' is likewise rather too neat for comfort.

The alternative conceptualization is of transracial adoptive identities as 'different but equal', a view most clearly articulated by Simon and colleagues. 'As young adults, the black adoptees stressed their comfort with their black identity and their awareness that they may speak, dress, and have different tastes in music than inner-city blacks – but that the black experience is a varied one in this society, and they are no less black than are children of the ghetto' (1994: 115). Like Feigelman and Silverman (1983: 170), Simon and Altstein (1987: 68), claim that the vast majority of transracial adoptees have a strong sense of racial pride and identification. However, they signally fail to explore the meaning(s) of black, implicitly lapsing into a crude empiricist view that 'black' simply means what black people (including transracial adoptees) do, think, and so on. Yet, 80 per cent of McRoy and Zurcher's (1983: 129) transracial adoptees reported having been told that they were 'not like other blacks', with many being said to 'act white'. Bearing in mind their tiny numbers, it seems highly fanciful to portray this as an 'alternative black identity'.

McRoy and Zurcher's study casts further doubt on the 'different but equal' view of racial identity. For despite overwhelming evidence of an association of transracial and same-race adoption with 'white' and 'black' orientations respectively, they found transracial adoptees more likely to use racial designations in self-description. McRoy and Zurcher argue that this derives from consciousness of physical dissimilarity and that cognitive acknowledgement of black identity is not matched by positive affect (p. 128, p. 140). Indeed, there is often evidence of discomfort on the part of transracial adoptees in relating to other black people (McRoy and Zurcher 1983: 108–9; Simon and Altstein 1987: 64; Ryburn 1994b: 67). McRoy and Zurcher's study (1983) is often quoted by supporters of TRA for its reporting of similar test levels of self-esteem among transracial and same-race adoptees. Yet, in reporting adoptive experiences they leave little doubt as to the greater 'ease' of same-race adoption in comparison with a more fraught TRA.[4] The 'black community' research often cited in support of TRA also shows a fairly pervasive scepticism regarding the 'different but equal' view. Even in the first survey by Bagley (Bagley and Young 1979), when there was said to be 'complete acceptance' of TRA shown by 71 per cent of black interviewees,

64 per cent stated that children lost their black identity in a white home, a figure which had risen to 79 per cent in 1989. Moreover, a majority of respondents thought the children would grow up failing to understand other black people and be prejudiced against them (Bagley 1993: 256–63).

If the 'having it all' scenario on self-esteem and racial identity can safely be laid to rest, we are left with how to make sense of the claims that disjuncture between the two can coexist peacefully – or, as Tizard and Pheonix (1994: 94) put it, that negative feelings about racial identity can be held alongside positive views of self. It has been argued here that the research findings of 'independence' are questionable, especially in their 'hard' form. The multifarious sources and foci of identity and the ability to compart-mentalize experiences should not be underestimated. However, the notion of clear separation is surely of concern on the basis of both psychological and ethical judgements. A strategy based on 'exceptionalism' – or belief that the black transracial adoptee is unlike other black people – would seem to be a vulnerable one. This is seen most dramatically when adoptions break down (Harper 1994), but is probably of enduring relevance throughout the life course. Moreover, even if such a strategy 'works' for some in mental health terms, there remain profound ethical questions on policy which the pseudo-science of adjustment should not be allowed to obscure (Triseliotis 1991a: 6).

Adoption, age and the foundations of identity

Though occupying a relatively low profile within research into 'race' and adoption, questions of attachment and the building blocks of identity pro-vide an important backdrop. They also form a key component in the liberal paradigm's broader support for TRA. These foundational elements comprise the quality of early parenting, love, warmth, security and consistency in relation to rules, norms and place in the world (Bagley 1993). The context for this is provided by the view that same-race adoption policies often threaten attachments either through delays or unnecessary separation when a child is removed from a white foster home (Golombok 1994). The priority of attachment over racial identity is asserted both negatively and positively. In the former case, it is argued that without the basic security which comes from attachment, the child will be beset with problems more serious than any arising from a lack of racial identity (Harris Hendriks and Figueroa 1995). Couched in more positive terms, good early parenting provides the base for personal identity and in turn for successfully tackling the difficulties posed by racialized social identity (Richards 1994).

These arguments, especially those on delay and separation, are arguably the most powerful for transracial adoption. However, as constructed within the liberal paradigm, they also carry certain dangers. This applies particularly to the over-separation of domains, as in Tizard and Pheonix's psychological and political (1989) or Richards's treatment of the personal and the social

(1994). In both cases, there is an appeal to a universal theory of individual human nature which can ultimately be understood separately from socio-political context. A more detailed critique has been offered elsewhere (Kirton 1995), but one example will suffice here. In support of his thesis, Richards (1994: 86) cites research by Kitwood into the identities of young British Muslims, arguing that their successful negotiation of competing demands and values shows family-based personal identity acting as a basis for social identity. Curiously, however, he overlooks the fact that the children's parents are not simply offering nurture, but socialization into Islamic mores and culture, i.e. a social base from which to explore identity issues.

Several of those supportive of TRA or ICA qualify their support by argu-ing that such adoptions may not be appropriate for older children with 'formed' identities, although they are likely to say this gives greater urgency to early placement (Gill and Jackson 1983: 138; Simon and Altstein 1987: 55; Bagley 1993: 139; Richards 1994: 86). Feigelman and Silverman's (1983: 100) multivariate analysis is used to show that placements which are delayed and/or involving older children give rise to far greater problems than trans-racial adoption.[5] Interestingly, however, in McRoy and Zurcher's study, the rather more positive outcomes of same-race adoption occurred in spite of the children being adopted at older ages into black families (1983: 23). If there is a certain common-sense logic behind early transracial placement in terms of continuity and the dangers of 'uprooting', it also raises awkward questions about the meeting of racial or ethnic identity needs. Tacit recogni-tion is given to the deep significance of racialized barriers, to racially diver-gent life courses and family patterns. Small (1986: 85) argues that Gill and Jackson's notion of a black self-image 'jeopardising the possibility of integration and emotional identification within a white family' betrays the assimilationism behind TRA. The difficulties of 'going back' are also high-lighted in the view that transracial foster care is more problematic than TRA (Triseliotis *et al.* 1995: 126), but again this raises wider questions about adoptees' (re)engagement with black communities. Given that the judgements to be made regarding the effects of delay or separation are always likely to be contested, there is also a danger in the Eurocentric view of attachment as focused on the nuclear family and the permanence offered by formal adoption (Gambe 1992). This might affect a range of decisions, from the desirability of adoption *vis-à-vis* other options to criteria for suit-ability on the part of adopters.

'No problem'? Adoptive families and the liberal paradigm

Research into the families adopting black and minority ethnic children has comfortably exceeded that focusing more directly upon the children, figuring in virtually all studies of 'race' and adoption. Reflecting the greater focus on transracial adoption, this research has been significantly weighted towards white families. Questionnaires and interviews with parents have not only sought to elicit information about the children but to chart parental experiences, attitudes and approaches to (adoptive) childrearing.

As perhaps the most obvious manifestation of failure, rates of breakdown (or disruption) in adoptive placements have been used as a rough guide to their success. Comparison of transracial and same-race adoptions reveals a mixed picture. In a review of disruption studies in the US, Festinger (1990) notes that most found no difference according to racial factors, with a small minority finding transracial adoption more vulnerable. Barth and Berry (1988), in a survey of 927 adoptive placements, found no difference in the rate of disruption. In the only large-scale British survey, Charles *et al.* (1992: 17–18) found that when other factors, such as age or length of time in care, were taken into account, transracial placements were a little more likely to disrupt, this being more pronounced for children of mixed parentage. Similar findings emerged from Berridge and Cleaver's study of fostering breakdowns (1987: 67). Overall, the evidence is suggestive of a slightly greater risk in TRA. Small clinical studies of disruption have raised issues of their more severe effects for transracially or transculturally adopted children. Harper says of inter-country adoptees that having acquired a new language and identity, the loss can 'render them a stranger in the world in which they find themselves, as well as in the world from which they came' (1994: 20). In similar vein, Rosenthal has written of 'triple jeopardy' faced by transracial adoptees, finding that previously unacknowledged racialized conflicts emerged after family break-up (cited in Bagley 1993: 80). Further evidence of vulnerability comes from McRoy and Zurcher's (1983: 146) finding that transracial adoptive families were much more likely to be referred to counselling services than their same-race counterparts (see also Howe and Hinings 1987). Differences in terms of milieux and attitudes towards counselling would offer at best only a partial explanation, while, significantly, McRoy and Zurcher found the referral rates higher among those living in predominantly white areas.

Study of transracially adopting families has revolved around four main issues. The first is that of motivation to adopt transracially, the second, integration of the adopted child within the family. The third and fourth cover interconnected questions of (racial) identity, namely the impact of family upon the child's identity and (dis)continuities in the identities of other family members.

Motives for transracial adoption

The significance of racialization poses potentially awkward questions regarding motivation for transracial adoption. If it is a response to the non-availability of white children will this 'second best' have adverse effects? If a black child is specifically sought, are the parents attempting to 'make a statement'? If 'race' is said not to matter, does this represent a dangerous 'colour blindness'? Ladner, who describes motivation as 'the most perplexing and controversial aspect of transracial adoption' (1977: 39) provides the fullest examination. She highlights the great diversity in motivations and circumstances within which parents became transracial adopters. Ladner found that adopting a black child was rarely the starting point but developed through varying mixes of parental response to the availability of black children and prompting from adoption agencies. Within this diversity, there was a common tendency for parents to be quite socially aware but rarely political activists. Child-centred motivations predominated, although these clearly coexisted with a wide range of views on the salience of 'race'. We will return to this below, but it is worth noting Ladner's concern over those who saw it as being of little relevance (p. 49). Most other studies of transracial adoption deal only tangentially with questions of motivation. Feigelman and Silverman (1983) locate transracial adoption within a broader pattern of families being politically left of centre, and 'less traditional' in their lifestyles, including gender roles. Although the importance of social and political awareness is widely recognized, there seems to be a consensus that wanting another child should be the prime motive rather than turning adoption into a 'cause' (Simon and Altstein 1987: 52). Many transracial adopters are said to be self-confident and inner-directed, showing a relative lack of concern for the (disapproving) attitudes of others (Ladner 1977: 29; McRoy and Zurcher 1983: 12). It must be said, however, that beyond such generalities, knowledge of motivation for transracial adoption and especially its effects, remains very sketchy.

One of the family?

The question of integration arises from hypothesizing that racialized barriers may diminish the mutual sense of belonging between a black child and white family, by comparison with same-race adoptions, black or white. Most research studies have found such fears unfounded (Gill and Jackson 1983: 41; Simon and Altstein 1987: 69). Yet, as elsewhere in the liberal paradigm, the claims are not as unassailable as the authors suggest. For instance, Simon and Altstein found transracial adoptees 'closer' to families than were white adoptees, but they do not explore the obvious implication of defensiveness or anxiety born of social isolation (1987: 74). They also claim to find evidence of integration from the similarity of perspectives expressed by adoptive parents and children but perform some mental gymnastics to do so.[6] Even where there is evidence of 'integration', its basis remains largely unexplored.

Relationships involving siblings and extended family members have been little examined in Britain but have figured significantly in United States studies. Though sibling conflicts can sometimes take racialized forms (McRoy and Zurcher 1983: 54; Austin 1985: 165), white siblings have generally been found to be supportive of black adoptees, particularly in a protective role outside the home and often in the face of receiving racist abuse themselves

Gill and Jackson's view of this is not without its own elements of rationalization. Acknowledging that it would be easy to criticize, they point to the 'paradox' of transracial adoption. 'The parents are encouraged to support and emphasise the "differentness" of their children. At the same time, as adoptive parents, they see one of their main tasks as making the children feel an integral part of their family', going on to say that not surprisingly parents opt for the latter (1983: 70; see also White 1985: 22). Parental fears surrounding differentiation leading to rejection have never been systematically explored, but have often emerged in passing (Bagley and Young 1982: 91; McRoy and Zurcher 1983: 38; White 1985: 17). As one mother in Jackson's study said of instilling racial pride, 'Suppose we encourage this and then he becomes a leader of Black Power and rejects us as parents altogether?' (1976: 20). Children too of course may have fears about being treated differently within the family, especially if this is done insensitively, or experienced as 'contrived' (Ladner 1977: 130; Austin 1985: 105). Gill and Jackson's paradox evokes Kirk's (1964) famous principle of 'acceptance of difference', but whereas Kirk boldly called on adopters to engage with the 'difference' of their adopted children, Gill and Jackson are all too ready to accept the lack of engagement with racialized difference shown by adoptive families in their study. In all major studies of TRA, evidence suggests that this is limited for most adopters, with relatively few responding to Ladner's call that they should 'identify not only with their black children but also with blacks generally' (1977: 140). McRoy and Zurcher (1983: 130) designated 60 per cent of white families in their study as 'colour blind', and only 20 per cent acting as 'interracial families' with strong black networks. No British studies have indicated significant numbers of transracial adopters living in multiracial communities. Too frequently, acceptance of difference is interpreted simply as accepting the racially different into the family, rather than as requiring at least some moves in the direction of a 'black lifestyle'.

Reconfiguring families?

In one of the few attempts to gauge identity changes within adoptive families, Simon and Altstein found the most frequent shift was from self-identification as white to being part of the 'human race'. Elsewhere, this form of discourse has rightly been challenged as a form of denial or means of dealing with racial ambiguity (Ladner 1977: 113; McRoy and Zurcher 1983: 140). Many transracial adopters believed that they had become more racially sensitive, while a few admitted to realizing how prejudiced they had been and sometimes still were (Ladner 1977: 97–8). While there are clearly positive aspects to this process of 'white growth', it also raises awkward questions about whether there are other equally prejudiced but less open parents, and more importantly whether such growth is taking place 'at the expense of the child(ren)'. The role of transracial adoption in promoting awareness for white siblings is also sometimes highlighted (Ladner 1977: 193), with Simon and Altstein in particular, keen to promote their view of transracial adoption as a crucible for social change. They note approvingly that white children in transracially adoptive families are more likely to have black friends, dates and so on than other white children. However, the effect seems relatively slight, only 6 per cent of their study group indicating that their best friend was black (1987: 63). The dominant aspiration in most adoptive families seemed to be towards 'colour blindness', a perception often shared by the minority of transracial adopters who have been active in multiracial networks (Ladner 1977: 142; Day 1979: 109; Austin 1985: 104; White 1985: 20).

Networks and localities – ethnic geography and adoption

Although the relationship between the two is extremely varied, it is clear that 'community' offers an alternative set of influences and possibilities to those of 'family'. Having noted the prevailing 'white' orientations within transracial adoptive families, it is pertinent to ask whether the effects of locality act to compound or offset them. As Gill and Jackson note, location, along with information on 'race' and its significance, is a key aspect of parental power. In their own study they found contact with black people limited or non-existent, with few 'taking race into account' in friendships. None of the families interviewed had moved to multiracial areas, though some had moved away from them in order to escape the prejudice and 'trouble' found there (1983: 59–60). Similarly, in the United States, white families have been much more likely to move to white areas than to multiracial ones (McRoy and Zurcher 1983: 103). 'The parents were aware of the need for greater contact with blacks, but could not make the final commitment to altering their lifestyles' (Johnson *et al.* 1987: 50).

Parental accounts provide several variations on the theme of exceptionalism at the level of community or neighbourhood. In many instances, black children are more 'acceptable' in white communities in the limited circumstances of having white parents and being few in number (McRoy and Zurcher 1983: 31): 'Once the neighbours realised that Darryl was here to stay and that no other blacks were moving into the neighbourhood or visiting him, they seemed to calm down' (p. 105). Not only is the absence of black people seen as soothing to the white community psyche, it is also taken to assist integration into families, as 'definitions of, and significance attached to, racial background in the families were not challenged' (Gill and Jackson 1983: 134). Exceptionalism is likewise discernible in the indifference or even opposition on the part of many transracial adopters towards more black families living in their areas (Ladner 1977: 255; McRoy and Zurcher 1983: 113). Ryburn's contention that on 'race' issues, transracial adoption frequently combines psychological denial with socio-geographic retreatism seems apposite here (1994b: 70).

There may, of course, be a certain protective value in such strategies, whereby playing the game of exceptionalism is rewarded by a lack of overt hostility and sometimes honorary white status. However, questions might legitimately be raised about who is being protected, from what and at what price. It is instructive to compare the ethno-geographical perceptions of black children in adoptive families and those of parents. McRoy and Zurcher's study of same-race and transracial adoptees found that while none of the former wanted a change in racial composition of their neighbourhood, half of the transracial adoptees expressed a preference for a more racially mixed environment (1983: 114). Simon and Altstein offer a different form of comparison, showing that while 72 per cent of white parents thought their children would wish to live in all-white areas, only 27 per cent of their black children agreed (1987: 90). Although, as we shall see below, Simon and Altstein have their own distinctive interpretation, these findings suggest that many adoptees are uneasy with exceptionalism and isolation from other black people. The identity tasks faced by minority ethnic children in 'white' areas are made difficult by the absence of markers of collective racial identity and direct experience of diversity among black people. If these problems exist for all families, including black adopters living in 'white' areas (Gill and Jackson 1983: 124), they are almost certainly accentuated by membership of a white family. Where there are few other black people or those of similar ethnicity, they tend to take on an undue significance, sometimes an attraction, more frequently as figures to be avoided (White 1985: 13; Husain and Husain 1996). Identity sources are likely to revolve around 'honorary white' status,[7] and a 'black' identity constructed either from paternalism or through 'humorous' play on black stereotypes.

Whatever the advantages in terms of 'getting by', such bases are scarcely good preparation for a multiracial society. Tacit recognition of the problem of isolation comes from the common desire to adopt more than one child transracially and while the resulting bonds are often very strong and supportive to the children, they beg questions of other familial relationships and of such privatized solutions (Jackson 1976: 14; White 1985: 21; Simon and Altstein 1987: 41). More generally, when social geography has been taken into account in studies, multiracial environments have tended to be found positive for both adopted children and families, especially in relation to racial identity (Grow and Shapiro 1974: 124, 166–7; Jones and Else 1979; White 1985: 8; McRoy 1991: 59). 'The sense of race pride, interest and identification, and the absence of a sense of shame, among black transracial adoptees are linked to the experience of integrated areas' (Feigelman and Silverman 1983: 105).

Class acts

Social class has always been central to formal adoption and there is little doubt that links with the liberal middle class have contributed significantly to the 'success' of transracial adoption. First, supporters can point to educational and career achievements (Dale 1987: 22; Morgan 1998: 70), while Bartholet has spoken of how TRA provides both material advantages and those of social capital. She counters the 'survival skills' arguments of critics with the claim that 'whites are in the best position to teach black children how to manoeuvre in the white worlds of power and privilege' (1994: 168). Within such views, class privilege serves a dual purpose, overcoming racial disadvantage through social mobility and providing a degree of protection against the effects of racism. This allows racial identity to be played down without denial of the significance of racism. A second factor is that class position offers presentational skills, including those within research interviews. It is interesting to speculate how favourably TRA would be regarded if it was generally the preserve of working class white families.

While clearly there are other important differences in play, it is relevant here to consider the overwhelmingly 'bad press' given to private fostering, where widespread neglect of racial and cultural identity issues has not appeared to be otherwise compensated for (Save the Children 1997). One of the immediate ripostes would be that racial awareness is much greater among the liberal middle class, and there is probably some truth in this. However, it also needs to be recognized that such 'awareness' is not necessarily translated easily or directly into child care practice (Raynor 1970: 164; Milner 1983: 115). Social class is also relevant to ethnic geography, with family location in 'white' areas and with correspondingly white social networks often explained largely as class effects. It may further be argued that critics of TRA often operate with an unacknowledged working class view of 'authentic blackness' and that middle class black families may be just as likely to occupy 'white' locations (Gill and Jackson 1983: 124; Tizard and Pheonix 1993). If there is some justification to this view, it is also the case that it fails to engage with the complexities of black middle class life, its similarities with and differences from white variants (Daye 1994; Small 1994). The articulations of class, 'race' and ethnicity remain little explored within debates on adoption, a reflection of the widespread unease over class among protagonists. On the one hand, writers within the black radical paradigm have shown little interest or willingness to explore black heterogeneity on class or indeed other grounds. On the other hand, beyond occasional attacks on the contradictions of the black radical position, liberal coverage has largely been confined to an implicit use of class to explain the success of TRA. For most liberals, there is an awareness that greater emphasis on class in this context would only serve to highlight the combined effects of class and racial inequality, providing ammunition to those who cast TRA as based on exceptionalism, paternalism or even 'child snatching'.

Culture, heritage and the liberal paradigm

The context for treatment of culture and heritage within the liberal paradigm has been significantly shaped by the black radical charges of assimilation or even 'cultural genocide'. The term culture is, of course, open to many different interpretations – from customs and the arts through to values, worldviews and 'ways of life'. Although most of the major research studies include some consideration of culture, there is little exploration of its meaning or complexities. Implicitly, understandings tend to constellate around either a self-evident racialized version – black/white culture – or an approximation to the 'museum' view, focusing on study and appreciation, perhaps of history or artistic forms.

In many respects, the handling of culture within the liberal paradigm mirrors that of racial identity, for which indeed it often serves as a marker. Once again, recognition in principle of the importance of acquaintance with, or knowledge of, 'culture of origin' sits uneasily alongside research evidence which purports to show its irrelevance to the success of adoption (Gill and Jackson 1983: 139; Zeitlin 1996). For adoptees, the primary focus has been with their interest in, or attitude towards, 'culture of origin'. In an early study in the United States, Grow and Shapiro found a fairly wide spread of views towards heritage, with 33 per cent exhibiting pride, 43 per cent indifference, and 24 per cent negativity (1974: 188). In Britain, both Gill and Jackson (1983) and Bagley (1993) have found relatively little interest expressed by transracial adoptees in either the museum or lived varieties of culture. Much more attention has been devoted to parental approaches which have in most studies been found to influence significantly the children's level of engagement and interest (Feigelman and Silverman 1983: 106; Gill and Jackson 1983: 79; McRoy and Zurcher 1983: 130). Paralleling the colour blind approach of many families to racial identity, the monocultural has prevailed in the cultural domain. This has resulted more often from 'qualified recognition' than deliberate and consistent strategy, a pattern detectable in the declining efforts made over time (Feigelman and Silverman 1983: 155; Johnson et al. 1987: 54). Simon and Altstein give the fullest account, attributing decline to lack of interest shown by the children: 'As the years wore on, as the children became teenagers and pursued their own activities and social life, the parents' enthusiasm and interest for "ethnic variety" waned . . . in the absence of signals that the activities were meaningful to their children, the parents decided that the one-culture family was an easier route' (1987: 109). For anyone who regards 'culture' as important in the context of children's needs, it is surely disturbing to see responsibility for parental motivation given to (dumped upon?) the children in this way. The defensiveness of Simon and Altstein's protestations is striking: 'Although many transracially adoptive parents do not go to any special lengths to emphasise their children's cultural identity, there are some who make a special effort to do so. Furthermore, even if adoptive parents do not vigorously and repeatedly reinforce the cultural identity of their non-white children, their action – or inaction – is not tantamount to a denial of their culture' (1987: 7).

It is also clear that except for the small minority of white families with strong multiracial networks, culture is largely restricted to what can be 'taught' rather than 'lived', with all the attendant limitations.[8] Feigelman and Silverman (1983: 107) emphasize the importance of socialization over the 'museum' view of culture, while Tizard and Pheonix (1994: 95) concede the impossibility of 'a person in one culture being able in any meaningful way to transmit another culture'. As for racial identity, the difficulties may also be exacerbated where efforts are seen as 'contrived/inauthentic', and/or are resisted by children as 'differentiating' (Ladner 1977: 115; White 1985: 15; McRoy 1991: 57). Overall, while many supporters of TRA strongly assert the possibility of white families meeting the 'cultural needs' of adopted children, there is little evidence to suggest that the majority do so. This applies even more to inter-country adoption where attention to issues of culture faces greater barriers (Hill 1991: 21), and assimilationism may be stronger and less subject to extra-familial challenge. An unacknowledged assimilationism may also help to explain certain curious silences within the liberal paradigm. One such is the area of language, which is so important in terms of identity and culture yet receives virtually no attention in the main research studies. This applies not only to acquaintance with birth parental language(s), but even to the first names given to children by their adoptive parents, which in many instances will also serve as a clear marker of adoptive status. A second neglected area is that of religion, which tends only to appear in discussion regarding (Christian) parental motivation (Grow and Shapiro 1974: 202; Simon and Altstein 1977: 62; Feigelman and Silverman 1983: 46). Raynor's discussion of its role in matching within the British Adoption Project is a small exception to this pattern, but the significance for adoptees of religion, whether that of the adoptive or birth family, is rarely if ever considered. In Britain, the omission is particularly glaring for children of Asian origin, for whom religion is likely to be (perceived as) a key marker of identity (Yawar 1992; Singh 1997; Abdulla 1998).

Arguably the major weakness, however, in the liberal approach to culture and related matters is a failure to locate them within a context of interaction, positioning and power relations. The preference within most families for at most the 'museum' view is uncritically replicated within research methodology and interpretation. Charting cultural dynamics is of course a highly complex task and examining their relevance for adoptive families even more so, but it is a matter of concern that little attempt has been made to engage with this task.

Locked in the incident room – racism and the liberal paradigm

One of the major charges levelled by critics of TRA has been that adoptees do not acquire the necessary coping mechanisms for survival in a racist society. Such coping is seen to rest on strong racial and cultural identities but also on acquisition of particular skills and techniques. Coping and 'survival skills' will be discussed further in the following two chapters, but at this point attention is focused on their treatment within the liberal paradigm.

Neither those undertaking nor (with occasional exceptions) those participating in research have denied the relevance of racism for (transracial) adoptees and their families. However, various manoeuvres are performed which serve to play down its significance and to rebut the view of racism as the Achilles heel of TRA. Some of these manoeuvres – such as a widespread 'colour blindness', the protective effects of social geography and class, or the foundational view of personal identity – have been alluded to earlier. Above all, however, the potential threat posed to TRA is contained via a reductionist understanding of racism in terms of particular incidents. Name calling is by far the most commonly reported type of incident, although other examples of hostility and rejection also figure on occasion (Gill and Jackson 1983: 102; Johnson *et al.* 1987: 50; Simon and Altstein 1987: 87).[9] The general impression conveyed is of incidents which are neither particularly common nor of any great consequence to the adopted children. Racial abuse is often characterized, both by adoptive parents and sometimes by researchers, as being on a par with other name calling (Austin 1985: 102): '*Being called a "Paki" may only be equivalent to being called "four-eyes" or "fatty"*, but it may still hurt' (Jackson 1976: 17) (emphasis added). Whatever the intentions, the effect of this or similar responses and interpretations can be to minimize or even trivialize the impact of racism. As Mallows (1991: 91) suggests, 'it is virtually impossible for a white person to understand the black experience, although it *is* possible to discount that experience by making false comparisons'.

There are several factors affecting adoptees and their parents which may lead to an under-reporting of racism. From the adoptees' point of view there may be inhibitions about reporting experiences of racism to parents (or researchers) and equally importantly conveying their subjective impact. Actual and even potential under-reporting have only rarely been acknowledged in liberal research (Jackson 1976: 14; Gill and Jackson 1983: 102; Lesley 1996), but the difficulties for black adoptees confiding in their white parents have been noted elsewhere (Younge 1994; Thompson 1996; Hayes 1996a) and borne out in our own interviews (see Chapter 4). They appear to rest on the perception that parents will neither be able to understand nor identify with the experiences. Such a view may evoke a protective response from the child who believes that the parent 'could not cope' with the experiences (Hayes 1996b). While communication on racism may be far from perfect in black families, the likelihood of such barriers is much less. As White (1985: 25) contends, 'the black family has a shared experience of racial discrimination so the child will be less likely to feel ostracised as a consequence of racial abuse'. In the only study to make direct comparison, McRoy and Zurcher found adopted children in black families talking much more with their parents about racism than their transracially adopted counterparts (1983: 37).

The processes involved in (mis)communicating about racism are complex and it may be that parents are more aware and receptive than their children imagine in this as in many other areas of family life. However, there is also strong evidence that many white families adopting or fostering minority ethnic children find racism an uncomfortable, even threatening phenomenon (Mullender 1988b: 189; Kelly *et al.* 1989: 33). The resulting defensiveness applies to acknowledgement of societal racism but perhaps more so to the (inter)personal level (Mallows 1989). As noted earlier, there are some transracially adoptive parents who are willing and able to open up regarding their own prejudices but closure and denial are far more common. In the words of one of the more open adopters, 'most white people are scared to face the powerful reality of racism and try to deny it; and of course, for white adopters this is even more threatening, and thus denying it even more likely' (Austin 1985: 104). From her small-scale study, Yaya (1994: 13) describes the inability of many adopters to appreciate the seriousness of discrimination as 'alarming'. What emerges more broadly from the TRA research literature is that within the great diversity of family life, the majority tendency is towards an atmosphere where racism is little discussed and that the driving force for this comes from parental attitudes, often unconsciously expressed (Sawbridge 1988: 9). There are occasional glimpses into the silences and their effects, as when members of an adoptive family describe how once they had opened up to their child's experiences of racism, they found the level 'astounding' (Austin 1985: 105). There is also, however, the problem of pain to which loving parents may be oblivious, and which may be hidden beneath the surface of success in education, employment and sociability (Hayes 1996a: 179).

Parental attitudes and awareness go beyond questions of communication and in particular affect their children's capacities to recognize racism, with greater awareness sensitizing children to discrimination (Grow and Shapiro 1974: 177; Wilson 1987: viii). This is especially relevant to the more subtle and/or 'institutional' forms of racism (Tizard and Pheonix 1993: 105). Raising awareness is of course neither straightforward nor an unequivocal blessing. Yet few would dispute that the risks of a strategy based on denial and avoidance – lack of protection, lost potential for collective support or ability to challenge – usually far outweigh any possible gains. It is also important not to confuse denial as a 'chosen' strategy or one copied from others vulnerable to racism with that which arises from ignorance or the need to coexist with white and therefore fundamentally different forms of denial.

In conclusion, the treatment of racism within the liberal paradigm remains severely circumscribed. The underlying problem is a rationalist construction of racism as prejudice and overt discrimination, the supposed relative absence of which requires no further scrutiny. Little attempt is made to lift the lid imposed by colour blindness and the effect of the research paradigm is to tighten it further. It is difficult not to see the net effect of such closure as silencing the voice of adoptees. To judge from the major research studies, self-reflection on the part of adopters seems comparatively rare, and its absence is rarely challenged by liberal researchers. One example of this is that the perceived protective effect of living in 'white' areas is rarely questioned. Yet, in one of the few studies to examine this in the context of transracial adoption, Grow and Shapiro (1974: 196–7) found adoptees facing more racist abuse in white areas, while a recent survey by Childline found minority ethnic children in predominantly white schools to be at greatest risk of racial harassment and bullying (Miller 1996).[10] Here, as elsewhere in the liberal paradigm, there is a pronounced circularity, with reluctance to 'make race an issue' serving to confirm, reassuringly, that it is not.

Lessons from racially mixed relationships

As was seen in Chapter 1, children of mixed parentage have been the group most likely to be adopted 'transracially' (Charles *et al.* 1992; Dance 1997). With rare exceptions, there seems widespread acceptance in the liberal paradigm that children of mixed parentage are black or seen as black. Hence, their adoption into white families is accepted as 'transracial' in ways which would not be used to describe their adoption into black families. In early studies, mixed parentage figured in two main ways, the first of which related to parental preferences and perceptions linked to a 'naturalized' colour gradation (Raynor 1970; Grow and Shapiro 1974; Simon and Altstein 1977: 81). A second focus was that of adoption agency practices on 'matching' and the notion that mixed parentage children were more appropriately placed with white families than other black children. Little attention has been paid in adoption research either to 'mixed' identities, or issues of 'dual heritage' as they might specifically affect transracially adopted children of mixed parentage. It should, however, be noted that most major studies of 'race' and adoption predate the small but growing research interest in children of mixed parentage (Wilson 1987; Tizard and Pheonix 1993; Katz 1996) and mixed relationships. This interest has provided a point of comparison for TRA (whether involving children of mixed parentage or not) and many within the liberal paradigm choose to see TRA and racially mixed families as variations on a common theme of 'inter-racial living' or 'mixed families' (Ladner 1977; McRoy and Zurcher 1983; Katz 1996).

At an abstract level, the similarities are cast in terms of overcoming barriers, transcending racial divisions and striking a blow against racism. Bagley gives the clearest expression of the coupling and progressive thrust, arguing that just as criticism of mixed marriages is reactionary, so too is that of TRA (1993: 247). Research studies do indeed reveal many areas of correspondence between racially mixed families and TRA. In both situations, there is frequently opposition from both white racists and racial or ethnic 'separatists', while parents and children may experience hostility from white and black sources. Those involved are also likely to face curiosity and innuendo and may experience awkwardness regarding 'explanation' of their situation. Rosenblatt *et al.* (1995: 168) observe how this may draw the children more closely to their parents, echoing the defensive closeness observed earlier among transracial adoptees. Other similarities have been found between white people who enter mixed relationships and those adopting transracially, including their relative independence and concern to broaden horizons (Rosenblatt *et al.* 1995). Katz (1996: 27) suggests that choice to enter a mixed relationship is far from random, while for Benson, albeit writing in an earlier era, it represents a 'political act' (1981: 13). As with transracial adoption, the opportunities for 'white learning' are noted within mixed relationships (Rosenblatt *et al.* 1995: 257). Class and social geography as mediating and contextual factors have been found important for mixed relationships, as have opposition from extended family members and the role of children in helping to overcome this (Rosenblatt *et al.* 1995: 96; Katz 1996: 162). It should of course be noted that, as with transracial adoption, great diversity has been found in all these areas and vital strengths found amid and through pressures.

For supporters of TRA, the value of these correspondences lies in their naturalizing influence. Articulating TRA with the growing and widely (if not universally) welcomed phenomenon of racially mixed relationships can serve to draw the sting of opposition. If the growth is progressive and 'natural', surely Bagley is right in declaring opposition to TRA 'reactionary'. There are, however, two sets of problems with this line of argument. The first, and relatively minor, difficulty is that by no means all the correspondences revealed in research into mixed relationships and children of mixed parentage have positive implications for TRA. For children, these include frequent 'exceptionalism', 'honorary whiteness', and greater discomfort in relating to black people (Benson 1981: 74; Wilson 1987: 168; Tizard and Pheonix 1993: 67; Rosenblatt *et al.* 1995: 92). Particularly where white parents (usually mothers) have had the central role, there has often been a gap between (self-)designation of the child(ren) as black and any practical meaning. Benson (1981: 138) terms this 'identity without content', while Katz notes that efforts to highlight black cultures have often been 'somewhat forced and self-conscious' (1996: 110). Studies have also found that participation in mixed relationships is no guarantee of freedom from racism, that conflicts are often racialized and that the threat posed by racism tends to keep its discussion off the agenda in many families (Benson 1981: 89; Rosenblatt *et al.* 1995: 40, 247).

The second and more serious problem rests with the coupling of mixed relationships and TRA itself. Notwithstanding their similarities, they represent very different social phenomena for two reasons. The first is that relationships between adults cannot be equated with those between adults and children. Although the former are mediated by a whole range of social forces, the presumptions of mutuality and 'free choice' can be taken as applying in ways which clearly do not hold for adoption. A second factor is that this power difference is not in any way offset by transracial adoption of white children into minority ethnic families. This 'one-way traffic' again clearly differentiates TRA from the situation of mixed relationships where

the reality of what the child *actually is*' (p. 88) (emphasis added). Evidence of injurious effects comes from examples of clinical work – or what Cohen (1994: 64) terms 'atrocity stories' – which are portrayed as fairly typical of work undertaken in relation to TRA (Maximé 1993: 176). Small and Maximé are also clear about the necessity of a 'positive black identity' for self-esteem, with the former attributing the decline in 'misidentification' directly to the growth in black consciousness. Small contends, albeit from personal experience, that misidentification does not take place in black families (1986: 88–9). As to the possibility of a black child forming a positive identity in a white family, Small's verdict is that this is 'possible, but rare' (p. 93). This view flows from his analysis of the motivations of white families adopting black children – such as those of 'rescue', 'making a statement' or the 'neo-colonialism' of some adopters who have lived abroad. The successful families are those who are willing to acknowledge and welcome the child's ethnic identity, are secure in dealing with racism, accept the transformation of their family lifestyle and are 'open' to black communities (1991: 66). Small's phrase 'black families in white skins' serves not only as a salute to these families, but also as an indirect way of highlighting their rarity (1986: 89).

The importance of racial identity and the difficulties faced by black youngsters in white homes have been common features of the professional child care literature in Britain (Pennie 1997). Commentary on the identities of transracial adoptees has usually taken place in the context of either specific case material or support groups, and is linked in various ways to 'identity work'. The logic of identity work is rooted in rejecting the (over-)separation of personal and social identity, and the related split between self-esteem and racial identity, and in the perceived need to 'feel good about being black'. Identity work may take the educational/social form of group work aimed at 'consciousness-raising' (Mullender 1988a; Mallows 1989; Hayes 1996b), or employ the psychological techniques of nigrescence (Maximé 1993), or 'cognitive ebonization' (Banks 1992). This literature offers a stark contrast with that of mainstream research on 'race' and adoption. Both the 'lack' of racial identity and, more so, its consequences are heightened. In her report on the Ebony Project for transracially fostered children, Mullender describes how the young people began by attempting to present as streetwise and with strong black community links, but that these claims tended to evaporate (1988a). Small similarly talks of the wearing of a black mask 'fiercely but weakly' (1986: 93). The problems are traced fairly directly to family experiences. Sawbridge (1988: 9) writes that as a result of unconscious racism adoptees experience 'a mixture of anger, sadness and bewilderment, and an awareness of being black without understanding what that means except in appearance'. By contrast, black families are seen as able to deal with identity issues without becoming 'over-zealous' (Brummer 1988: 79). For Peters, black parents 'are careful to put pride in racial identity in proper perspective so that it becomes neither an obsession nor a crutch' (1985: 165).

Racial and ethnic identities – assessing the claims

Although the advocates of same-race adoption clearly draw upon 'black psychology', this does not generally take the form of detailed reference to research findings. Yet the latter do provide the basis for scrutinizing some of the arguments more closely, notably in illuminating patterns of identity development for children growing up in black or minority ethnic families. Of particular interest are those studies which examine patterns of identification and their links with self-esteem. Many offer critiques of the doll tests and psychological testing methods similar to those discussed in the previous chapter (Harrison 1985; Aboud 1987; Rosenthal 1987; Jackson *et al.* 1988). Harrison (1985) notes the hidden influence of white norms, as when white same-race preference is extrapolated into a general principle, against which any expressed white preference among black respondents is treated as 'self-hatred' rather than as reflecting a more biracial orientation. Those who favour Africanist views of 'self' are particularly critical of the use of universal measures of self-esteem (Akbar 1985; Harrison 1985; Nobles 1988).

The relationship between racial or ethnic identity and self-esteem for black children which featured so strongly in the liberal paradigm has been extensively studied with somewhat variable results. Findings range from those that have found a positive correlation between strength of racial identity and self-esteem to those that have found no relationship or a negative correlation. To some extent, these variations reflect the difficulties of adequately measuring either racial identity or self-esteem before any relationship can be considered (Jackson *et al.* 1988: 247). Beyond the problems of measurement, research findings are not quite so contradictory as they at first appear. There is for instance substantial consensus around the view that black children must deal with negative social imagery and hostility and that the solidarity provided by a mixture of family, peer group and community is important in helping them do so. Most studies have found high levels of self-esteem among black and other minority ethnic children and have explained this in terms of an ability to 'compartmentalize' experiences in ways which protect against negative social forces (Harrison 1985; Jackson *et al.* 1988). Families in particular are often described as providing a buffer or insulation (Spencer 1987: 114). 'Black families emphasise rearing their children to be comfortable with their blackness – to be secure, to be proud, and to grow up being and feeling equal to anyone else' (Harrison 1985: 189). Also highlighted are the importance of respondents' reference groups and the values which underpin their sense of self (Rosenthal 1987; Jackson *et al.* 1988).

Perhaps the major problem rests with the construction of any measure of racial identity which does not implicitly equate its 'strength' with militancy, distance from white norms and conformity to racial/ethnic stereotype. Yet as Phinney and Rotheram (1987: 102) contend, healthy identities may cover a range of orientations from militancy to assimilation. Cross (1987) develops this argument further. (Re)assessing identity changes during the black revolution, he considers that 'upon reflection . . . it did not seem logical that pathology was typical of "Negro" identity and mental health was the province of "Blackness" '. In a way which seems to echo liberal constructions separating personal and social identity, Cross takes the former as a proxy for psychological health and stresses its lack of any necessary association with social identity: 'Black identity is not predictive of personal happiness, but it is predictive of a particular cultural–political propensity or worldview' (1987: 126). Of transracial adoption, Cross states that black children raised by white parents are no more or less likely to be psychologically healthy than those raised in black families but are likely to have different world-views (p. 133). While he attacks romanticized views of ethnic identity as a panacea, Cross does acknowledge that an assimilationist world-view may mean isolation from black people who are not assimilated (p. 133). He also argues that, while individual black people may find meaning in life divorced from other black people, the black community requires a 'critical mass' to ensure its survival (p. 127).

What then might be gleaned from such research and theorization for adoptive identities? It must first be noted that wider research into the relationship between self-esteem and racial identity underscores many of the concerns expressed in Chapter 2 about the ultimate usefulness of the exercise. In relation to racial identity, the major pitfall remains that in the desire for measurable scientific data, it is treated as an individualized characteristic, rather than as something more contingent and 'situational'. Despite his recognition of the consequences of assimilation, it is argued here that Cross drifts in some respects into such reified views of personal and group identities. In particular he fails to convey that group identities operate within parameters and boundaries (albeit loosely and sometimes contentiously defined). Heterogeneity within those parameters, i.e. there being many different 'black identities', does not preclude the possibility of identities which fall outside the parameters of 'blackness' – perceptions of which are signified in the derogatory language of oreos, coconuts, and so on. It is questionable whether any 'continuum' view of racial or ethnic identity does justice to this 'break', and no study (to the author's knowledge) adequately addresses this methodologically, despite widespread recognition that the drawing and maintenance of boundaries are central to notions of identity. Crucially, too, the bases from which orientations evolve must be considered. Thus it is dangerous to equate the 'assimilation' manifested by those raised in black families with that developed in white families. These stances are likely to have been reached by different routes, derive from different experiences, and reflect different motives and patterns of attraction and distantiation. Though not necessarily so, assimilation is likely to be more of a 'chosen' orientation for the children of black families, in terms of their own and/or parental choices. In either case, the choices are likely to be more open and explicit.

Implications for the black radical paradigm are difficult to gauge because its adherents do not explicate their understanding of black identity/ies.

Implicitly, a 'self-evident' view is proffered, as in the notion that children must have a 'positive black identity'. While there is an important kernel to this argument, it has often been dangerously over-simplified (Banks 1999). In relation to black adopters, two contrasting images are in circulation. The first is that families are expected to share the wider black radical conscious- ness of the paradigm. The second is that heterogeneity is, if not positively welcomed, at least accepted, perhaps partly on the pragmatic grounds that (prospective) adopters may not always be among the most politicized and that highest priority is given to racial or ethnic matching (Rhodes 1992: 230; Bagley 1993: 256–63). Unfortunately, there is no research evidence which casts light on this issue. What is clear, however, is that to posit neat correlation between black identity and self-esteem represents a gross simplification.

Culture and heritage in the black radical paradigm

Arguments for same-race adoption have drawn strongly on issues of culture (or heritage), although this has rarely involved any detailed discussion of its meaning or interpretation. While the distinction is not always clearly held, it is possible to detect two distinct strands of thinking in relation to the importance of culture for minority ethnic children and families. The first is couched in the language of rights, with an identifiable culture or heritage seen as a 'birthright'. The second is more contingent and casts culture as a resource, the importance of which derives from its place as a social marker and, for minority cultures, the threat of devaluation relative to the majority.

The birthright view has gained a wide currency, in part reflecting a broader interest in genealogy and 'roots'. Article 20 of the UN Convention on the Rights of the Child 1989 states in respect of decisions on adoption or foster care that 'due regard shall be paid to the desirability of continuity in a child's upbringing and to the child's ethnic, religious, cultural and linguistic background'. (This phrasing is also used in the 1989 Children Act, section 22(5), for consideration of children's needs.) In relation to adoption in Britain, official guidance issued in 1990 indicated that 'all children should be encouraged and helped to understand, enjoy and take a pride in their ethnic origins and cultural heritage' (SSI 1990: para. 11). There are, however, important tensions linked to the birthright view, both in its interpretation and its linkages with the more contingent view of culture or heritage. Wider currency has helped break down the ethnocentric view that only the Others have cultures – which can studied, evaluated, and perhaps manipulated or managed from the security of an unquestioned Centre. Recent debates over that historically most invisible of cultural identities – 'Englishness' – give a powerful indication of this trend towards the need for greater scrutiny and self-reflection (Alibhai-Brown 1997). Yet, such developments also carry certain dangers, especially the neglect of power in the evolution and interrelation- ship of 'cultures' which can easily create a false equivalence.[1] Relatively more powerful groups are often able to impose, directly or indirectly, their cultural forms on subordinate groups and to exert greater control over cultural exchanges and flows. In the contemporary context, there is also scope for 'me-too' strategies, whereby members of more powerful groups cast themselves as disenfranchised victims in a society which has (supposedly) granted rights to all its minority groups (Waters 1990). Thus, it can be argued that official endorsement of the birthright view comes at the price of a political accommodation, namely that issues of power, hierarchy and social critique are safely banished to the margins.

The resource view is set within the context of culture's use as a means of domination, with subordinated cultures systematically inferiorized, denied or even eliminated (Fanon 1965: 168). (Attempted) cultural domination is met with resistance. Marable (1995: 118) contends that 'when culture is constructed in the context of oppression, it may become an act of resistance', while for so-called cultural nationalists, central importance is given to 'cultures of resistance' in giving the oppressed a collective identity (Omi and Winant 1994: 42). The special significance of the cultural sphere may derive from its provision of spaces which are more readily available to oppressed people, not least because cultural resources are more difficult to control than material ones (Goldberg 1993: 110; Small 1994: 13). A particular example cited by Gilroy is the strong link between expressive culture and struggle under slavery (1993: 57). As a historical exercise, the (re)claiming of culture requires a wide-ranging contestation of the 'view from above' i.e. history as written by the 'oppressors'. More specifically, this entails not only laying bare the 'realities' of cultural domination and its various rationalizations, but importantly charting the modes and paths of resistance. The resulting 'sense of history' is widely seen as a powerful antidote to many of the effects of oppression and as an inspiration to continued struggle (Edelman 1988; Nobles 1988). The danger that culture may be construed in static terms and interest in it become an exercise in nostalgia is often emphasized by activists (Biko 1988). For Fanon, the only true culture is in the (revolutionary) making. 'It is around the peoples' struggles that African–Negro culture takes on substance, and not around songs, poems, or folklore' (1965: 189). In the somewhat less revolutionary theatre of western capitalism, the struggle has largely been one for recognition – seeking a shift which Johnson (1988) describes as being from cultural deviance to cultural variant within a pluralistic society. However, the (de)politicization of culture remains an important issue, with activists expressing concern about culture serving as a form of retreat, an opting out of struggle (Omi and Winant 1994; Marable 1995: 194).

As an institution, family often occupies a vital place within the broader treatment of culture. It can be regarded both as the conduit for cultural transmission and, in its particular form(s), as a manifestation of cultural tradition (James 1981). Black families have been cast as more egalitarian and child-centred than their white counterparts (Glick 1988; J. McAdoo 1988: 259). They are also found to have greater extended family involvement in childrearing and to have more elastic boundaries which may include non-related 'fictive kin' (Day 1979; Dodson 1988; Daly *et al.* 1995: 245). In similar vein, other writers have set out what they see as the differences from white western familial norms for those of South Asian and Chinese origin (Dwiwedi 1996; Lau 1996). Within the family, cultural norms may be conveyed relatively unconsciously. In a process which they call 'tacit socialization', Wade Boykin and Toms argue that cultural styles and values are transmitted and absorbed through day-to-day encounter and are not dependent upon conscious articulation or directives to learn (1985: 42). Rosenthal (1987) describes this socialization process as creating a 'boundary from within' – an interpretive frame through which to view the world, the 'correctness' of which may be little challenged.

Within the black radical paradigm, the divergence of minority cultures from the mainstream is accentuated, especially in relation to values and behaviour. Black and white value antithesis is portrayed partly in oppositional terms deriving from racialized divisions, but Africentric perspectives describe value systems where differences are more pervasive and deep-rooted. White European individualism, competition and secularity are often contrasted with African emphasis on the group, cooperative solidarity and spirituality (Daly *et al.* 1995). Akbar (1985) argues that the former's values have in effect been normalized within psychology, shaping developmental expectations in matters such as delay of gratification or expression of affect. Lived cultural differences are also evident in a wide range of behaviours, cognitions and hence presentation of self. Robinson (1995: 29–45) offers a summary of such 'differences' in gaze/eye contact, touch, personal space, emotional display and carriage as well as clothing, speech and manners.[2] Language is particularly closely linked to culture as both medium of expression and boundary marker. In her study of French- and English-speaking Canadians, Heller (1987) shows how language shapes (the terms of) entry into social relations and their subsequent development. She argues that 'shared language is basic to shared identity, but more than that, identity rests on shared ways of using language that reflect common patterns of thinking and behaving, or shared culture' (p. 181). Kochman (1987) distinguishes between what he terms the emblematic and non-emblematic in language, with the former carrying significance in boundary marking or maintenance. Writing of black Americans, he notes how language serves as a means of judging (in)authenticity and group membership. Language differences may, of course, encompass those of established languages and/or more subtle, improvised forms based on vocabulary or speech intonation.

The significance of 'cultural differences' for identity is open to competing interpretations. On the one hand, it can be argued that in a pluralistic society they are relatively peripheral to people's lives, neither bestowing great rewards nor damaging through constriction. Moreover, as the acquisition of culture occurs through socialization, it might also be suggested that there is no necessary 'primordial' link to culture simply through accident of birth (Malik 1996: 150). According to Macey, 'an individual's physical appearance seen in the context of previous under-representation and it should be noted that even as same-race policies have become more established, the number of black social work managers has fallen (Thompson 1997). It is also clear that black support for same-race adoption and many of its key propositions is much more widespread than can be explained away by 'removal from the constituency' (Bagley 1993: 256–63; Kirton 1998).[1] As to Gilroy's charge of statism and the confounding of autonomous self-organization, this too does little justice to the complexities of either black political activism or welfare provision, and sounds all too reminiscent of the traditional Marxist cry of 'revolution betrayed'.

Of greater significance than the merits of Cohen and Gilroy's arguments, however, is their location within debates on adoption. For their critical fire is directed overwhelmingly at the black radical paradigm, while the liberal paradigm largely escapes interrogation or receives tacit endorsement. Thus, while Cohen's account of the 'fundamentalist' battle between new right assimilationism and black nationalist separatism is aimed at creating space for a post-modern transcendence it equally leaves the way open for liberalism to offer a progressive 'middle way'. His claim that black children in same-race placements are 'just as likely to invent imaginary white companions' (1994: 71) as those in white families is not only empirically unsubstantiated but fits conveniently with the symmetrical topography favoured by liberal positions on 'race'.

The sense of arguments coming 'full circle' to liberalism is also evident in Gilroy's contributions. As a highly respected black sociologist, he is clearly a prize catch for the supporters of transracial adoption (Gaber 1994: 28). His implicit alignment is made clear in his Foreword to Gaber and Aldridge's (1994) *In the Best Interests of the Child*. Despite its being (with the partial exception of Cohen's contribution) a straightforward restatement of the liberal paradigm stretching back at least two decades, Gilroy describes the collection as a 'rich and provocative book . . . (which is) . . . long overdue and desperately needed' (1994: ix). Gilroy has little to say about what constitutes this richness, perhaps not surprising when the book has sufficient 'coat of paint' theorizing on 'race' to take care of the Forth bridge. In common with his other forays into the world of adoption (1987: 64–7; 1992), Gilroy is very clear on what he opposes, namely the ethno-dogma surrounding 'same race' adoption, but extremely hazy on what he favours. The 'transcendence' rather than conservation of racial identities (noted above) goes unexplained, raising the suspicion that it amounts to little more than the traditional 'boundary-crossing' argument of the liberal paradigm. The suspicion deepens when Gilroy states that same-race policies are 'hotly defended with the same fervour that denounces white demands for "same race" schooling as a repellent manifestation of racism' (1992: 58). Not only might this have been penned by any liberal writer, but it seems extraordinary that someone of Gilroy's sophistication can collapse the contradictions between supremacist and defensive 'separatisms' in this way.

This 'paradoxical' endorsement of the liberal paradigm is linked to the wider relationship between post-modernism and liberalism which, despite their profound differences on the centring of individuals, share considerable common ground (Best and Kellner 1991: 288). Both are hostile to macro-level theorizing, of systemic, totalizing analysis, favouring the more localized and pluralistic. Both are individualistic – liberalism openly so, post-modernism largely by default. The commonalities mean that post-modernism and (neo-)liberalism can coexist peacefully but, as Larrain contends, this is because the former offers no serious challenge to the latter (1994: 17). Indeed, it might be argued that this elision reflects the wider 'defeat of socialism' and a scaling down of radical aspirations.

Assessing the post-structuralist challenge

At the heart of the post-structuralist challenge lies a call to recognize the power of destabilization and uncertainty, of transformed social relations and the need for new ways of understanding them. This impacts most strongly on the black radical paradigm which is taken to ground support for same-race adoption in 'essentialist' or 'primordial' views of racial identity and cultural heritage. If these views are found to be inadequate or outmoded, so the argument runs, the case for same-race adoption policies becomes fatally flawed (Macey 1998). We will return to this proposition below, but it is important to contextualize it by examining the broader critique offered by post-structuralist thought.

In the theoretical domain, several writers temper their critique of essentialism with recognition of the weight of history and of social structures. For Brah (1992: 143), while identity is never a fixed core, 'changing identities do assume specific, concrete patterns, as in a kaleidoscope, against particular sets of historical and social circumstances'. Connolly similarly emphasizes the ever-present tension between the achieved and ascribed and the 'multiple and deep channels' linking personal and collective identities (1991: 161). Beyond such qualified support for the post-structuralist project, there is also a deeper concern over its political direction and claims to radicalism. Critics point to a 'fragmentation without end' which undermines social categories and hence the basis for political action (Gabriel 1994: 178). One of the major problems with the debate around (anti-)essentialism is that it has for the most part been carried out in highly abstract, theoretical terms, often incorporating a crude dichotomy of open/closed identities (Parker 1995: 232). There is, however, a small but growing body of empirical work which has engaged with the post-structuralist problematic (Mama 1995; Parker 1995; Alexander 1996; Back 1996). Examination of this (and other closely related studies e.g. Hewitt 1986; Waters 1990) facilitates not only assessment of the patterns of continuity and change suggested by post-structuralism, but also some of the issues core to debate on 'race', ethnicity and adoption. It will be argued here that although this research provides some supporting and interconnection. The pitfalls of binarism and the idealization of black families and communities are real and must be guarded against. Diversity and interconnection are also closely linked to the cross-cutting of 'race' and ethnicity with other forms of social identity, whether of class, gender or age – mediations which require careful consideration. Finally, the critique stands opposed to psychological simplification, whether in the suppression of psychodynamic ambivalence or the potential crudity of imposed 'identity work'. As Patel (1997: 185) suggests, the latter must be 'about exploration rather than indoctrination or glorification of any culture'.

Having acknowledged these pitfalls, it is also important to point to certain dangers within the anti-essentialist critique and its application to adoption. The greatest of these is of a zero-sum logic which infers that, if concepts do not have a clear and uncontested meaning, they have no meaning at all, or that any interpretation is as valid as any other. Deconstructing 'fixed' meanings can easily lead to an undue emphasis on fluidity which loses touch with lived experience. Similarly, stress on uncertainties and contingencies can disguise the lived experience of structured continuities, including the (future) impact of racialization upon the lives of black and minority ethnic people in Britain. This is not a question of 'the same old story' but one which recognizes that social change in such a deeply ingrained area is unlikely to be very rapid, and is far from certain in its direction. The post-structuralist quest for 'openness' has been directed almost entirely at the perceived 'closure' represented by same-race adoption. Yet, not only is this 'closure' largely mythical (who presents adoption of white children into white families in this way?), but it seems to overlook the more profound closure which can divide transracial adoptees from other black experiences and 'communities of origin'. Overall, while lessons must be drawn from 'anti-essentialism', they do not provide a basis for radical departure from same-race adoption policies. Although in matching terms, the latter must be understood in terms of providing a 'loose fit' rather than a rigid mould, the case for a 'secure base' from which to explore and negotiate remains strong.

Having set out the case for a continuing emphasis on same-race adoption, we turn in the final two chapters to the broader agendas of child care policy and of links between adoption and the politics of 'race' and ethnicity.

5

'Race', adoption and the child care system

In the previous three chapters, we have looked at particular perspectives on 'race', ethnicity and adoption largely in terms of (individual) children and families. We now turn to consider the relationship between adoption policy and practice and the wider child care system of which it is part.[1] On the one hand, this linkage means that issues of 'race' and ethnicity in adoption must be located within that broader context. On the other hand, it is important to examine the former's impact upon different aspects of child care practice. In this chapter, we will start by addressing developments in child care as they relate to 'race' and ethnicity, and then consider various aspects of adoption policy and practice more directly.

Given the guiding principle (enshrined in the 1989 Children Act) of maintaining children in their own (birth) families where possible, adoption is customarily viewed as the end point of a process in which such efforts are deemed to have failed or have been ruled out as inappropriate. The practice and decision making involved is as difficult as it is politically charged. Direct participants in the process must grapple with decisions over when, and under what circumstances, plans to keep or reunite children with their families are to be abandoned. Managers and policy makers must also decide what resources should be committed to such efforts. In both instances, there is a need to balance the risks of precipitate removal with those of 'drift'. As was noted in Chapter 1, adoption lies at the heart of the struggle between family rights and 'permanency' perspectives. Views range from those who see little or no place for adoption in its current 'closed' form (Family Rights Group 1984; Ryburn 1994b) to those who would accord adoption a clear 'social engineering' role, with the public care system acting as a conduit for the transfer of children from 'underclass' to middle class families (Morgan 1998).

Although these and other protagonists would construe the 'road to adoption' in radically different terms (Fox Harding 1991), all would recognize its starting point in the worlds of 'preventive' family support and child to the closed model was most advanced), through autobiographical writing (Shawyer 1979; Inglis 1984) and the pioneering research of Winkler and Van Keppel (1984). In this work and the several volumes which followed, various myths were shattered. These included the notion that relinquishment was in any meaningful sense 'voluntary', with most mothers feeling that they had no choice or were effectively coerced into the adoption (Bouchier *et al.* 1991; Wells 1993; Logan and Hughes 1995; Mason and Selman 1997). Perhaps an even more important myth to be exploded was that the clean break benefited birth mothers – allowing them to 'get on with their lives'. For the constant theme in all accounts is that the losses and pain associated with relinquishment rarely disappear or even diminish, sometimes intensifying with the passage of time (Bouchier *et al.* 1991: 60; Wells 1993: 23–4). What has also emerged clearly is the way in which such difficulties were exacerbated by professional practice and lack of any (ongoing) support. While issues such as 'saying goodbye' to children are generally handled much more sensitively today, the quality of services given to relinquishing parents remains patchy and often inadequate (DoH 1992). It must also be noted that while birth mothers have come at least partly out of the shadows, the same cannot be said for birth fathers (Clapton 1997), siblings or extended family members (Tingle 1994; Mullender and Kearn 1997).

'From social pressures to legal judgements' – contested adoptions

While the changing social climate surrounding illegitimacy has contributed to more sympathetic views of birth mothers relinquishing children for adoption in the 1960s and 1970s, the same may not be true for birth families whose children have been adopted *during* the 1980s and 1990s. As noted earlier, adoptions are increasingly likely to be from the care system and to be contested i.e. take place without the consent of the birth parents. Contested adoptions rose from the almost negligible during the 1960s to account for approximately 30 per cent of all adoptions (and 57 per cent of 'freeing' applications) in 1995 (Charlton *et al.* 1998: 3).[2] Increasingly, those who lose their children through adoption are more formally and publicly being judged as 'unfit' parents. The pain of losing a child against their will is added to all the other losses experienced by birth parents. While it is clearly important not to romanticize the latter, contested adoptions have been criticized, especially for their adversarial nature. Ryburn (1992) has charted the ways in which social work agencies, once they have decided to pursue adoption against parental wishes, will gather and present evidence in ways which maximize the likelihood of 'success', magnifying parental failings and putting the most favourable gloss on social work actions. The high 'success' rate, at well over 90 per cent (Murch *et al.* 1993: 28), suggests that social work accounts are usually accepted by courts, while crucially they also shape the information subsequently available as case records. Whatever the merits of the decision on adoption, this has the twin effects of 'adding insult to injury' for birth parents and prejudicing information available about them in future, including to their child(ren). Two further effects of the adversarial process are that parents tend to be excluded from any role in planning for the child's future, thereby working against the 'partnership' philosophy of the 1989 Children Act, and that they receive little if any support in relation to their loss through adoption (DoH 1992; SSI 1993: 32; Charlton *et al.* 1998).

For Ryburn (1994d) these issues raise fundamental questions about the institution of adoption itself, especially in its closed form, which turns contested adoptions into 'winner takes all'. Not only do birth parents suffer considerable injustices but, according to Ryburn, the adversarial process works against the interests of all those involved in the adoption triangle, making the management of transitions and future relationships much more difficult. He advocates the replacement of contested adoptions with negotiated arrangements – modelled along the lines of Family Group Conferences – which would facilitate wider involvement from extended family and significant others, and promote greater openness, so that substitute care need not mean severance of contact with birth family.

'Race', ethnicity and birth families

As in other aspects of research into child care, the experiences of black birth relatives in adoption have received little attention. There are, however, important observations to be made both from the fairly limited information available and wider knowledge of the child care system. Howe *et al.* (1992: 35) note that despite the growing literature on birth mothers, and the controversy surrounding transracial adoption, 'the black birth mother has not yet spoken', a verdict that is as applicable to domestic adoption as to intercountry adoption. A report from a Post-Adoption Centre birth mothers' group does make reference to white mothers with children of mixed parentage and their concerns about experiences of racism within transracial placements.[3] To date, however, there have been no attempts to explore either the contribution of racism to relinquishment, or how different cultural traditions may impact on experiences of it.

Contested adoptions involving black and minority ethnic families raise other important issues. These include the possibility that the adversarial process may enshrine ethnocentric judgements, whether on the part of social workers or the courts (Banks 1994). Ryburn (1994d) cites a case of an African–Caribbean mother's 'obsession' with plaiting her transracially fostered child's hair being used as evidence of her unsuitability as a parent. Charlton *et al.* also suggest that, for black parents, the perception of them as parental failures carries a different significance when the decision makers are white (1998: 109). Dispensing with parental consent is based on what a 'reasonable parent' would do,[4] which, irrespective of 'race', is an extremely fraught area, replete with value judgements. In a thoughtful paper, Lawson (1994) raises interesting questions regarding the hypothetical 'reasonable parent', and in particular whether, and in what ways, 'race' is taken into account in her/his construction. Under what circumstances, for example, would an objection to transracial placement be '(un)reasonable'? On the limited evidence available, minority ethnic parents also appear less likely to access post-adoption support services (Howe *et al.* 1992; Charlton *et al.* 1998).

Yet arguably the most far-reaching questions arising from 'race' and ethnicity relate to adoption itself, or rather its exclusive western form. It is widely recognized that closed adoption is culturally alien to most of Britain's minority ethnic groups, if in different ways. For those of African descent, the traditions of adoption are much more informal and open, while for many South Asian communities the problems relate to adoption by strangers, and in the case of Muslims to formal adoption *per se* (Vyas 1993; Jordan 1994; Ryburn 1994c; Fratter 1996: 30). Similar issues apply to many of the 'sending' countries in inter-country adoption (Dutt and Sanyal 1991; Ryburn 1994b: 71–3; Mullender and Kearn 1997: 9). The dangers of imposition relate both to the severance of contact with birth family and to the prioritization of adoption over foster care. For while the prevailing Eurocentric wisdom is that adoption is generally the superior form of substitute family care, black families often prefer foster care, partly for reasons of financial and other supports, but also because of unease regarding closed adoption (King 1994). In sum, it might reasonably be argued that many of the difficulties inherent in current institutional arrangements for adoption are likely to impact disproportionately upon minority ethnic children and families. Additionally, the difficulties are likely to grow the more vigorously adoption is pursued within the child care system (Morgan 1998).

Towards open adoption?

Moves towards greater openness in adoption in the past two decades are closely linked with the critique of closed adoption outlined above.[5] Impetus has been gained from recognition of the part played by birth families in meeting the identity needs of adoptees, the pain experienced by birth relatives and, perhaps more controversially, the potential benefits to adopters who develop more 'inclusive' relationships with birth family members (McRoy 1991; Triseliotis 1991b). Openness can be seen as building on moves to make it easier for adoptees to trace, search for, and reunite with birth families. If such possibilities were advantageous in adulthood, why not during childhood? A professional practice deeply imbued with the assumptions of the closed model has been slow to embrace openness, particularly in relation to direct contact, being sceptical regarding its value and hyper-aware of its potential to destabilize the adoption. The fears have not been borne out by research studies, either from countries, notably in Australasia, with longer experience of open adoption, or from Britain (see Ryburn 1994b and Fratter 1996 for reviews).

Research on openness in the context of race and ethnicity is as yet limited. This is especially so in the case of tracing, searching and reunion (although an ongoing research project by the Children's Society will help to rectify this). In a preliminary study, the society found that 11 per cent of adoptees seeking information about birth relatives were black or of mixed parentage, a figure difficult to interpret due to lack of statistics for comparison, and the varying dates of adoption (Feast and Howe 1997). Given, however, that all the adoptions considered would have taken place no later than the early to mid-1970s, and many much earlier, it suggests at least a fairly high interest on the part of the adoptees involved. By contrast, a survey of birth family members registering on the Adoption Contact Register found a very low level of minority ethnic involvement, around 1–2 per cent which, among other things, may reflect continuing alienation from the bureaucratic trappings of formal adoption. For inter-country adoptees (and often birth families), searching and reunion can be vastly more difficult because of the many barriers of geography, language, culture and record keeping (Ngabonziza 1988: 39; Hill 1991: 21–2). In the United States, Shireman (cited in Simon *et al.* 1994: 93) found greater interest in birth family from 'same race' compared with transracial adoptees. This finding is of course open to differing interpretations, notably according to whether it is taken as a sign of troubled adoptions or as healthy interest.

Qualitative data on the meaning and significance of various forms of openness is also thin on the ground, particularly in relation to issues of 'race' and ethnicity. From the limited evidence available, it is fairly clear that birth family contact takes on a particular significance for many transracial adoptees in relation to racial or ethnic identity (Feast *et al.* 1998: 57–61). Both supporters and opponents of TRA claim that moves towards openness strengthen their case. Craven-Griffiths (1994: 122) argues that openness can help meet the identity needs of minority ethnic adoptees in white families, a view which finds some support from Fratter's (1996) small-scale study. However, there is also substantial evidence that contact occurs more reguarly and works more smoothly when adopters and birth family share the same ethnic background (Loftus 1986; Barn 1993b; Fratter, 1996: 230). These two positions are not, of course, incompatible. Openness may well *both* improve the quality of transracial adoption *and* yet still work better within same-race placements. It should also be noted that, while openness is generally to be welcomed, it also carries certain dangers, particularly its use as a bargaining chip to persuade parents/mothers to relinquish their children (Triseliotis 1991b: 33; Van de Flier Davis 1995).

Finding families, challenging racism?

The 'supply' of black families for adoption or foster care is of crucial importance in several respects, with controversy over their (alleged) shortage almost as fierce as that surrounding identities. This debate is relevant not only to the 'necessity' for transracial adoption, but also to the performance of adoption agencies and their relationship with black communities. Although, as we shall see, some supporters of TRA have expressed concern over 'lowering standards', virtually no-one disputes the value of recruiting minority ethnic families or the very considerable advances made during the past decade or so. In this context, liberal support for TRA has increasingly come to focus on its offering a 'good second best', i.e. providing an effective alternative if the ideal of ethnic matching leaves children deprived of, or waiting an unacceptably long time for, an adoptive home. Many supporters of TRA are quite convinced of the shortage of minority ethnic families and that same-race policies have made deprivation and delay widespread if not endemic (Aldridge 1994; Macey 1995: 478; Triseliotis *et al.* 1997: 166). Such beliefs are pivotal to the liberal setting of 'race' against 'attachment' or even 'a loving family'. The politics of this will be discussed in the next chapter, but it must be acknowledged that issues of delay undoubtedly provide the most powerful weapon in the pro-TRA armoury. It is important, therefore, to examine more closely the 'reality' of shortage and its relationship to policy. As described in Chapter 1, the 'inevitablility' of shortage was challenged from the mid-1970s onwards, building on the Soul Kids campaign (ABAFA 1977) and early community-based projects (Ahmed 1986). The success of recruitment drives, especially in certain London authorities (Arnold 1982; Brunton and Welch 1983; Shroeder and Lightfoot 1983) had the effect of switching the spotlight from 'the problems of black families' towards a critique of adoption agency practice. The starting point of this campaign was to demonstrate the untapped potential in black communities, entailing, especially for those from the Caribbean,[6] the countering of images of family instability but above all of indifference (James 1986: 169). The long tradition of (informal) adoption in the African (and Asian) diaspora was emphasized, alongside the failure of child care agencies to acknowledge or build upon it (Ahmed 1986: 155; Coleman 1994). The critique of agency practice was wide-ranging, but the recurrent theme was one of lack of awareness – of black community life and more importantly the context of its relationship with state bureaucracy.

Recruitment efforts required the opening of communication channels and at least partial acknowledgement of black mistrust of 'officialdom' – as fact, as understandable, and perhaps even as justifiable. The new channels included targetted campaigns, use of 'ethnic' media and liaison with community groups, churches and so forth (Ahmed 1986; Kaniuk 1991). What was important in these approaches was their introduction of a new dimension to relationships between child care agencies and the black community. For the former, black families needed to be seen as resources rather than simply as 'problems', while the latter could see agencies in a more constructive light, and not merely as 'child-snatchers' (Stubbs 1987: 484). Assessment of families rapidly emerged as a key issue, in terms both of its process and the criteria by which applicants were deemed (un)suitable. Work to recruit black families served to highlight the problems of bureaucratization and their ethnocentric effects. First, most (potential) applicants were unused to state mediation within substitute family care and second, were likely to be mistrustful of it (Day 1979: 28). Recruitment campaigners in both the US and Britain soon realized that slow responses, police checks, and intimate questioning about personal and family life could easily be experienced in racialized terms and deter applicants. Equally important was the way engagement with black communities threw into sharp relief the parameters within which families were assessed and the way formal criteria were used to exclude them (Day 1979: 127; Stubbs 1987: 486). Traditional norms were particularly challenged by older applicants and single women, many in paid employment who often expressed a more direct interest in financial supports than agencies were used to (Rhodes 1992: 165).

Mirroring wider debates on the 'politics of the family', the acceptance of such applications is open to two very different interpretations. From the 'traditionalist' right, it reflects declining standards by lowering the thresholds for suitability, in effect approving families 'just because they are black' (Dale 1987; Bartholet 1994: 161; Morgan 1998: 115). For such critics (who are also keen to point out the lower incomes of black adopters/foster carers) the decline is a direct consequence of same-race policies, a misguided attempt to disguise the 'real' shortage of families and one which condemns black and minority ethnic children to 'second best'. An alternative view comes from the left, where the changes are seen as progressive, not only in relation to facilitating same-race adoption but as liberalizing the criteria applied to white families (Rhodes 1992: 257). This more positive encounter with 'difference' was seen as a catalyst for improved understanding of the children's needs in the context of familial heterogeneity. Thus, for the 'progressives', a more open stance on suitability combines the virtues of opportunity for a wider range of families with greater potential to focus on the (often special or unusual) needs of particular children.

Such claims are difficult to evaluate, in part because they rest heavily on value positions, but also because there has been relatively little research into the recruitment and, above all, the assessment practices of adoption agencies (Stubbs 1987). From the evidence which is available, it does appear that increased flexibility in criteria has to an extent been grafted onto, rather than replaced, earlier family norms. The preserved hierarchy relates not only to approval of adopters *per se*, but also to the pecking order for adoptable children. In broad terms, this means that children with less troubled histories are more likely to be placed with families which approximate the desired 'norm', while the more troubled are matched with 'less conventional' families (Simon and Altstein 1987: 128). In these circumstances, the consistent finding of successful adoption by (black) single parents is the more striking (Owen 1997; Triseliotis *et al.* 1997: 216).

The absence of systematic monitoring also makes it difficult to gauge the success of recruitment efforts in 'quantitative' terms. On the one hand, there is evidence that many urban authorities (especially in London) recruit minority ethnic substitute families in numbers which match the needs of their 'looked after' populations (Barn *et al.* 1997; Toor 1997). Barn *et al.* did not find evidence of children 'languishing in care' awaiting placements in any of their three local authority areas. On the other hand, a Social Services Inspectorate (SSI 1993: 30) report on adoption services in three northern authorities talks in almost matter of fact terms of the 'particular difficulties' faced in recruiting minority ethnic families, while Chambers (1989) has argued from a survey of *Be My Parent* (a book published by BAAF which advertises children for adoption) that black children wait much longer to find adoptive homes than their white counterparts. Wider surveys suggest that the variations are at least loosely linked to (ethnic) geography. Dance (1997) found very few transracial adoptions taking place in London or metropolitan boroughs but comprising over 50 per cent of minority ethnic adoptions in shire counties. Waterhouse (1997: 46) found a similar picture in relation to black foster carers, with few recruitment problems in London boroughs but very significant ones in shire counties. What these broad brush surveys fail to answer is how far the geographical variations simply reflect the ethnic composition of local populations as opposed to recruitment policies and practices, a question to which we will return below.

For their proponents, same-race policies have also served as a means for challenging aspects of institutional racism in two main ways. The first, referred to above, has been their fostering of a climate within which the strengths of black families are more likely to be recognized and black culture more valued (Arnold 1982). Second, it can be argued that they have served as a catalyst for change within child care agencies themselves. This relates not only to stimulating at least a measure of self-reflection regarding relationships with black communities (James 1986: 166), but also because successful recruitment of minority ethnic families has been seen as closely linked to the employment of workers from those communities. Especially in early recruitment campaigns, the gulf between agency and community appeared such as to require black and minority ethnic workers as 'intermediaries', promoting mutual awareness but perhaps more importantly helping to counter the image of a 'white' agency and the associated mistrust. With occasional exceptions (Schroeder and Lightfoot 1983), the active involvement of black workers has generally been seen as a prerequisite for effective recruitment and subsequent support of black substitute families (Day 1979: 35; Ahmed 1986: 157; Kaniuk 1991: 38; SSI 1997: 25). For those who support the 'vanguard' view of same-race policies, it might be contended that the establishment of black workers in family placement sections provided the base for their wider recruitment in child care work, representation in related bodies, such as adoption panels, and a broader 'educative' function within the agency (Arnold 1982; James 1986; Yaya 1994). As noted earlier, other writers have expressed scepticism regarding the vanguard thesis. Stubbs has noted that commitment to same-race policies does not necessarily mean salience being given to 'race' issues more generally (1987: 480), while in her case study of same-race policy implementation, Rhodes (1992) argues that despite the rhetoric of community involvement, practice was conservative and profession-led. Caesar *et al.* (1994), while clear about the contribution of black workers and their crucial presence for organizational change, also highlight the way this influence can be circumscribed and the workers 'pigeonholed' and exploited.

Given its central importance, how might the debate on the 'shortage' of minority ethnic families be summarized? As has been observed, the task is rendered difficult by the lack of research into recruitment practices and their efficacy. Two propositions will be advanced here, the first of which is to acknowledge the many weaknesses, potential and real, within the vanguard thesis. Collectively, these mean that none of the perceived benefits of same-race policies will necessarily ensue. Such policies may fail to deliver the right families at the right time and even where successful in those terms may divert attention away from broader issues within child care, notably preventive and child protection work and the context of poverty and racism within which they occur. Institutional reform and the position of black workers may remain firmly tokenistic – as indeed may same-race policies themselves. Yet the second proposition is this: that if we must be vigilant against any conception of same-race policies as both necessary *and* sufficient for effective adoption (and child care) services, care must also be taken to avoid slippage from the 'insufficient' to the 'unnecessary'. In historical terms, there can be little doubt that without the 'hard line' policies initiated in the 1980s, current numbers of minority ethnic adoptive families would be significantly lower. This view is supported at the national level by comparison between the early 1980s and mid-1990s, with transracial adoption having given way to same-race adoption as the majority form (Charles *et al.* 1992; Dance 1997). Similarly, although evidence at the local level is limited and fragmentary, there appears to be a significant correlation between those agencies which have taken the most determined stances on ethnic matching and those which are now best able to attain it (Heywood 1990; Waterhouse 1997: 46). This fits with a broader pattern of success for aggressive equal opportunities policies (Edwards 1995: 56).

While ethnic geography clearly has an impact in terms of availability of families and workers from minority ethnic communities, potential for community links, political pressure and so forth, agency success in recruitment is by no means reducible to these factors (Butt *et al.* 1991). The regular attacks on same-race policies as 'politically correct' have also been tacit demands for greater use of transracial adoption. Most (including that launched by Paul Boateng) have been accompanied by prefacing remarks endorsing efforts to recruit minority ethnic families. What is rarely acknowledged in this juxtapositioning is the (institutional) complexity of recruitment policy. The liberal compromise, advanced by Aldridge (1994) and others, is that ethnic matching is sought within an agreed time limit, after which transracial adoption should be utilized. At first sight a reasonable proposal, it crucially glosses over the extent to which institutional racism remains an obstacle to recruitment of black and minority ethnic families and what effect the introduction of 'time limits' might have upon it. Implicit in such approaches is the notion that the lessons have now been learned, both in relation to the needs of minority ethnic children and the recruitment of families, and that same-race policies have long ceased to be necessary, if indeed they ever were. Yet, the example of the successful initiatives to recruit minority ethnic families has demonstrated the extent of previous complacency and institutional racism; while the continuing regional variation in these initiatives indicates that shallow acceptance of the 'absence' of minority ethnic adopters is far from banished.

Relax? Don't do it!

The view proferred here is that the point has not yet been reached where any 'relaxation' of efforts to recruit minority ethnic families should be contemplated. The wider political context for this position will be explored in the following chapter, but in relation to child care and adoption practice can be briefly summarized at this point. Only the most staunch, assimilationist supporters of TRA would dispute the significant gains which have been made in the past two decades in terms of ethnic matching and awareness of the needs of black children. Yet the gains have relied heavily on the impetus generated by the black radical paradigm. By contrast, the liberal response has often been limited, grudging and resistant with an ever-watchful eye out for demons which must be exorcised (Ahmed 1986; James 1986). In her study of a London borough's introduction of a same-race policy for foster care, Rhodes says of white workers that, except for a few, 'attitudes ranged from ambivalence to open hostility' (1992: 64). It is noteworthy that, while supporters of TRA regularly indicate their support in principle for adoption by black families, their interventions have almost invariably been to characterize its pursuit as over-zealous and in practice to oppose it in specific cases. The crucial question is whether a decreased emphasis on ethnic matching would represent a consolidating move 'beyond' the gains already made, or simply a step back from them. Can it be ensured that the option of TRA is coming into play following the maximum possible efforts to secure an ethnic match? The evidence on this is not encouraging. An SSI (1996b) report found variable adoption agency performance, with some examples of good work, but often a lack of effective publicity (none of the authorities produced any material in minority languages) or liaison with community groups, and sometimes virtually no discernible attempts at minority ethnic recruitment. Such is the mythological power of hard-line same-race policies that in a later report, the inspectors appeared somewhat shocked at finding 53 per cent of minority ethnic adoptions into white families. They were moved to comment that far from the image of rigid same-race policies 'the converse may be true; that SSDs were not doing enough to secure same-race placement for children and they were being placed with white families by default' (SSI 1997: 28). Such a verdict is powerful given that the SSI (perhaps mindful of the concerns of their political masters) do not generally give a high profile to 'race' issues in their inspections and in particular fail to integrate it as a dimension when it is not directly in focus (Richards 1995). At the level of individual practice, Selwyn (1996: 18) found little attention being paid to issues of religion or culture in adoption reports prepared for court. Mention might also be made of the use of adoption allowances which, unlike in the United States, do not appear to have been used in the UK to promote adoption by black families. Indeed the survey by Hill *et al.* in the 1980s still found it far more frequently used in transracial adoptions (1989: 70).

In all these circumstances, it is difficult to believe that the majority of adoption agencies are currently pursuing the recruitment of black and minority ethnic families vigorously or effectively enough to permit the introduction of any relaxation without this having adverse effects upon an already inadequate level of performance. As Weise (1988) notes, while there are dangers in a 'grim determination' on the part of agencies to find black families, it is clear that such efforts suffer when this commitment is absent. Similarly, there is little indication of any changing notions of the qualities necessary for successful TRA. Thus, while measures to address delays are important, it is vital that they do not, even unwittingly, undermine the quest for ethnic matching. The problems attending same-race policies must be addressed 'internally', by those sympathetic to their aims, rather than by bureaucratic or juridical diktat, an argument which will be elaborated in the next chapter. External involvement should facilitate this process of reform within a strongly supportive environment. It is thus sad, but instructive, to note that under its Quality Protects initiative (DoH 1998b), the Labour government has not included any targets on recruitment of minority ethnic carers or on matching children with them alongside its targets for reducing delays and moves within the care system.

6

Adopting a wider-angled view

'It wouldn't matter if no black men went into teaching in the next
500 years so long as there were great teachers from other cultures.'

The date is October 1997, the occasion a public debate on Children and
Racism, organized by the Children's Society,[1] and the above a reply to a
question from the floor about the importance (or not) of greater black participation in teaching. The speaker is Head of Public Affairs at the BBC and
a Commissioner for the CRE. In the latter role, he tells the audience that he
is closely involved in a project on black men, seeking in particular to address
their poor record in responsibility, manifest in the arenas of family, work
and involvement in crime. Not only does he appear to take the evidence for
'irresponsibility' at face value, but he seems to draw no connection with the
positive roles which may or may not be available to black men over the
next 500 years. More generally, he expounds his philosophy on racial justice,
namely the need to move away from a focus on rights to one of opportunities
and obligations, from use of the law against discrimination to constructive
engagement with major corporations. His description of the BBC as a great
success story in this regard is hotly disputed by a black female colleague
who describes him as looking through 'rose coloured glasses'.

As you may have surmised, the speaker is a transracial adopter. Having
told his audience that he lives in Peckham next to a school where 46 languages are spoken, he uses the conference platform to launch an attack on
what is clearly one of the major forms of racism facing children, namely
same-race adoption, which he mistakenly describes as required by the 1989
Children Act. Happily at odds with the CRE's (1990) stance on adoption
he declares, 'I don't believe in asserting racial and ethnic identity as a
priority.' With the confidence of someone who believes they have a rightful
place at the heart of the debate, he tells of a recent 'discussion' with the
then Health Minister, Paul Boateng, and the Chief Social Services Inspector
about the need to speed up the adoption process, implicitly including much
greater use of transracial adoption. Whether this discussion contributed to
Boateng's subsequent outburst against same-race adoption one can only
speculate, but it would certainly not have discouraged him.

This vignette is included here because it highlights some of the themes of the chapter so well. In particular, it shows how powerfully the liberal 'grain' runs through transracial adoption at every level, from the familial to the institutional and political. In this final chapter, we will be looking at the relationship between adoption and the wider politics of 'race' and ethnicity. If adoption is far too small an area of socio-political life to exert major influence, it should nonetheless be remembered that it affects a significant number of people and has a symbolic value which allows it to punch beyond its weight as a public issue. We will therefore consider the question of what contribution policy and practice in adoption might make to broader social currents. The major focus, however, will be on the wider political domain providing the context within which adoption practice takes place, and policy is formulated. Particular attention will be devoted to the prevalence of liberal discourses and their framing of debate upon racism and racial justice.

Integration vs separatism

The capacity for 'race', ethnicity and adoption to generate controversy owes much to its resonance with wider debates regarding 'the nature of society'. Both TRA and same-race adoption are commonly portrayed as promoting and contributing to particular visions of society, practically and symbolically. The struggle has been billed, especially from the liberal camp, as one between the integrative thrust of TRA and the separatism represented by same-race policies. We will start discussion of this couplet by looking at the evidence advanced in support of the 'integration' thesis.

According to Bartholet, in a society torn by racial conflict, studies of TRA 'show human beings transcending difference' (1994: 169). Integration is seen above all in the family setting and the 'acceptance' of a minority ethnic child into a white family, but it also sends out signals that 'race' need not act as a barrier to caring, nor need it ultimately 'matter' in relationships. Simon and Altstein have been the most consistent advocates for the integrative potential of TRA. In their early work, the sense of its providing a crucible for social change is palpable when they write of producing colour blind individuals 'who will serve as the nucleus for a new community that does not perceive social differences on the basis of race and which does not identify individuals in traditional racial categories' (1977: 5). Interestingly, even Chestang, who played such a foundational role in the black radical paradigm, acknowledged that TRA had 'catalytic' potential. Predictably perhaps, evidence of the wider impact of TRA is largely confined to the symbolic level (including its bracketing with racially mixed relationships) although it is acknowledged as generating its own networks i.e. with contacts of transracial adopters going on themselves to adopt (Day 1979: 94; Austin 1985). Ladner also notes the argument that TRA is likely to promote rather than threaten black culture by drawing families into it and involving them in black struggles against racism (1977: 146). As was described in Chapter 2, evidence at the familial level focuses on the integration of the adopted child into the family and the shifts which occur for other family members. Simon writes of 'broadening experiences' for adoptive parents and the 'something special . . . (which) . . . seems to happen to both black and white children when they are reared together as siblings in the same family' (1994: 147).

Integration is, crucially, open to vastly different interpretations. Constructed along a continuum, it may signify at one end assimilation and at the other major adaptation to accommodate forms of 'difference' and to diminish or eliminate racialized hierarchy. Interpretations themselves are often racialized. Small (1994: 155) notes, for instance, that the level of black population required for perceptions of an 'integrated' neighbourhood is much lower for whites than for blacks. He also suggests that whereas whites tend to associate integration with harmony (or the absence of conflict), for blacks parity is relatively more important (p. 151). What quickly becomes clear in the 'integrationist' case for TRA is that definition leans strongly towards assimilation. Despite the references to a 'nucleus for a new community' or an 'interesting model' for better living, the limits of such possibilities are readily apparent. This is not only because of the small scale of adoption but also the obvious danger of drifting towards social engineering. For as long as transracial adoption occurs in one direction only, increasing its scale would simply exacerbate the tendency towards assimilation. If social transformation was always a touch ambitious, the prospects to go beyond assimilation would seem better at the familial level. Yet as analysis of the liberal paradigm has shown, the picture of TRA as a social phenomenon is one where assimilation remains the dominant influence, with clear exceptions to it very much in the minority.

This pervasive assimilation appears matched only by the tendency for liberal researchers and commentators to deny it by over-emphasizing the 'multiracial' elements in the lives of transracial adoptive families. What is revealed in such judgements is the power of white norms, against which TRA can be seen as self-evidently integrative, transcendent or even revolutionary. There is no doubt that families were taking a major step if this is judged against prevailing white attitudes. Yet in the absence of more adaptive forms of integration, the spectre of paternalism was always likely to haunt TRA. While some adoptive families have pointed the way to a more meaningful integration by 'letting their lives become entwined with those of black people and sharing some of their burdens' (Day 1979: 89), this has not applied to the majority, for whom integration has been largely confined to adopting a black child and aspiring to 'colour blindness'.

Although the construction of same-race policies as 'separatist' approaches an article of faith for their liberal critics (Aldridge 1994: 200; Bartholet 1994: 179), the case is as weak as that for TRA being integrative. It is heavily reliant upon the assumption that same-race policies are a direct reflection of black nationalist rhetoric about 'nation building' and its critique of TRA as ('genocidally') depriving the black community of its children. Bartholet further attempts to bolster the liberal position by contrasting it with the kindred currents of white and black separatism. This involves raising the extraordinary red herring that same-race policies are influenced by white separatist fears of white children being placed in black families (p. 179). Fanciful or not, such argument is useful in allowing the double equation, first of 'separatisms' one with another and secondly, of separatism with racism, to which we will return later in the chapter. Yet perhaps the major flaw in the liberal charge of separatism is the tendency to extrapolate beyond the family. The (false) coupling of opposition to TRA with that to racially mixed relationships has already been noted, but it is also claimed that it logically implies antipathy to integrated (i.e. racially mixed) education (Bartholet 1994: 172). Expressed by advocates of adoption, this seeming inability (or unwillingness) to recognize the centrality of parenting in the lives of individual children, by comparison with the more impersonal world of schooling, is strange indeed. It is also clear that schools can be ethnically diverse in ways which are difficult if not impossible to replicate in families. Paradoxically, far from 'implying' separate education, same-race policies have been premised (especially in Britain) on the expectation of, and as a counter to, inevitably strong 'white' influences upon children beyond the home. Interestingly, although the linkage with 'separate education' is intended to discredit same-race policies, a recent survey of black pupils found roughly 40 per cent of them indicating a preference for attending an all-black school, with experiences of racism given as the main reason (Meikle 1997).

While same-race adoption certainly fits comfortably with 'separatist' ideas, the link is by no means a necessary one. It is difficult to see what is 'separatist' about adoptees being brought up in a similar fashion to other minority ethnic children, with white schoolmates, friends, participating in 'white' institutions and so forth. If there is an element of separatism, it is in the exclusion of white parents but this assumes transracial adoption as a norm. It also highlights the way in which the charge of separatism is almost invariably levelled at the defensive strategies of relatively less powerful groups rather than the more widespread exclusionary practices of the powerful (Williams 1974: 318). Thus, the fact that black family adoption of white children remains largely 'unthinkable' has never been construed as evidence of 'separatism'. While liberal opposition to same-race policies is no doubt genuinely felt, it also serves, as Rhodes (1992) argues, as a defence of 'white' cultural hegemony and as a claim to care for minority ethnic children, as adopters or foster carers. None of this is to deny problems which may be associated with 'separatism', whether in the danger of 'sacrificing' the interests of individual children or simply question marks over its long-term viability and effectiveness as a strategy for promoting racial justice. Black 'autonomy' would seem currently less fashionable than a decade ago and is certainly no panacea. However, it is difficult to believe that its relative demise either reflects progress towards racial equality or makes it more likely. Though its form must always adapt, the underlying logic for a measure of

the dissenters. 'Counter-attack' is a central feature of coverage of 'race' issues within the media and, as such, is revealing of the 'raw nerves' of liberalism with respect to 'race'. The techniques will be described below, but will be prefaced by some observations about the underlying logic of argument, and the pivotal role played by deracialization. Although its processes have become naturalized to a degree, i.e. accounts are seen as 'objective' and proportionate in their value judgements on 'race', there is little doubt that deracialization is also used 'strategically' (Reeves 1983). Such is the absurdity of some commentary that it can only be explained in terms of knavery rather than foolishness. Deracialization is a multi-layered process, especially when considered as a form of denial – ponder for a moment the extreme rarity of anyone 'admitting racism' set alongside what is known about its extent (Reeves 1983: 189). As Essed notes, denial is crucial to covert racism, while to allege racism is to enter a minefield of resistance, rationalization and, importantly, counter-attack (1991: 150). Within liberalism, deracialization is regarded as diminishing or opposing racism, whereas racialization (including 'race talk') is viewed as exacerbating or promoting it (Reeves 1983: 175). Defining racism in this way allows a positioning of liberalism between different forms of racism, the overt variety of the far right and the 'anti-racism' of the left. Thus, denial of racism and denunciation of those who allege it go hand-in-hand (van Dijk 1993: 9). Whites do not offend blacks but vice versa through the accusation of racism (Essed 1991: 274). Given that racism is almost universally seen as blameworthy, shifting the blame from perpetrator to victim through the charge of 'reverse racism' becomes an invaluable device (Reeves 1983: 215; van Dijk 1993: 21).

This schema is of course presented too neatly. However, the implicit centring of liberal values marks out the parameters of moderation, the pale beyond which lies 'extremism' (Wetherell and Potter 1992: 166). One of the strengths of liberalism is its apparent openness, but this also involves setting the limits of 'legitimate critique', the exceeding of which brings responses decidedly illiberal in tone and often substance. The theme of 'tolerance under threat' is played out, 'we' have become too tolerant and 'they' are abusing it (van Dijk 1993: 76; see also Blommaert and Verschueren 1998). Genuinely felt and/or 'strategic', the resulting anger helps to explain the often hysterical tenor of the counter-attack, which serves as a warning to the critics and paves the way for reprisals against them. With the threat suitably exaggerated, the badge of courage is donned for the crusade against 'political correctness' (van Dijk 1993: 262).

Welcome to PC world

In this section, we look at the discursive techniques employed to 'close down the critique' (hooks 1992: 120) of TRA and white liberalism and to demonize their opponents. The underlying message is that of contrast, between those who have reason and compassion on their side and the interests of (black, albeit deracialized) children at heart, and those who manifestly lack such qualities and represent a serious threat, not only to children and adopters, but also to cherished values. Michael (1996) offers an instructive account of how the socio-ethical domain is constructed in the battle between moderation and extremism. He talks of the 'core set' and the Others who are excluded from it. The former's authority rests in particular on their claims to 'rational emotionality', a phrase denoting expertise based on technical knowledge but tempered by, and congruent with, emotional understanding. This balanced concept allows dismissal both of those who are 'unduly emotional' and the coldly technocratic who are oblivious to the human consequences of their 'logic'. While unobjectionable in principle, rational emotionality can easily be colonized in such a way as to deny legitimate critique, whether on 'rational' or 'emotional' grounds. In relation to adoption, the colonization is most evident in the demarcation between experts and 'alleged' experts. The proponents of same-race adoption have their 'expertise' ridiculed as having no real basis, being simply 'trendy', or 'fashionable'. Real expertise is mobilized from within the higher echelons of the 'psy' professions, as when the *Observer* (27 August 1989) provides the following mocking comparison of reaction to the court decision in the Croydon case: 'While the BAAF welcomed the decision and a black children's pressure group called it "wonderful", a *leading* child psychologist condemned the decision as Nazi-like and a *distinguished* child psychiatrist called it "institutional child abuse"' (emphasis added). Two features are of interest here. The first is that despite the absence of any track record in relation to adoption or issues of 'race'/ethnicity, the authority of these experts is seemingly beyond question. A second feature is the highly emotive nature of this (and much other) expert testimony. Such language is not ordinarily associated with 'expert comment' but, within the liberal construction of rational emotionality, is implicitly justified because of the 'evil' involved.

Building the case against same-race adoption policies entails the closure of certain discursive spaces and the opening up of others. The two crucial areas of denial are those of critique of TRA and any positive representation of same-race adoption. Closure is especially important in establishing that decisions and practices do indeed rest on political correctness (PC) (or its surrogates), by denying any alternative explanations and refusing to grant social work activities any conceivable rationale. For example, in the case of the 'racially naive' Lawrences, the ensuing investigation by the SSI found a range of concerns about rigidity in their attitudes towards childrearing and upheld the decision. Yet the mythology was clearly more attractive and was repeated regularly in following years, including by Conservative Health Minister Stephen Dorrell, who cited the Lawrences' case to justify the then latest 'crackdown' on PC, seemingly unaware or perhaps wilfully ignorant of his own inspectors' findings (*The Times*, 18 February 1997). More generally, the PC thesis is upheld by a mixture of crude over-simplification and outright misrepresentation. These tendencies are not simply evident in tabloid head-lines such as 'Blair to End the Adoption Scandal' (*Express on Sunday*, 12 April 1998) and 'Crazy Bans on Adoption to be Axed' (*Daily Mirror*, 28 August 1998). Even in the quality press, the impression of rigid adop-tion rules – above all on 'race' – goes unquestioned. The *Independent* (23 January 1998) talks of *Britain* operating a same-race policy, while the *Guardian* (29 March 1996) argues the need to relax the *iron rules* on 'race' and age. Yet, as noted earlier, recent research evidence (Dance 1997; SSI 1997) demonstrates clearly that TRA is still taking place on a significant scale, while the SSI report (1997: 35) found that roughly *60 per cent* of adopters were over the widely quoted 'age limit' of 40. Clearly, such minor details cannot be allowed to distract readers from the PC reality of adoption practice.

PC is also defined as the antithesis of 'common sense', which became the watchword for politicians during the 1990s. Of particular interest is the deracialization implicit in the term. When Stephen Dorrell states that 'deci-sions about who could adopt should reflect commonsense values widely shared by society' (*Guardian*, 18 February 1997), he is contending that the 'public' view – which accords little if any significance to 'race' – must prevail. Yet, the author's research (Kirton 1998) has shown quite clearly the divergence of white and minority ethnic opinion on the adoption of black children, a racialization of common sense that is conveniently ignored. A further quote from Dorrell echoes the 'love versus race' couplet discussed above: 'Any commonsense person would ask not whether a couple knew about racism but whether they could provide a secure and loving home for the children' (Laurence 1997). The two are apparently unconnected and verging on mutual exclusion – the idea that, in many hours of discussion, both might be assessed is ruled out. The deeper message is that of boundary maintenance, reasserting the 'irrelevance' of 'race' and offering reassurance that any complaints about its 'over-emphasis' will be upheld by those in power. It is noteworthy that 'over-emphasis' requires no benchmark, fuel-ling suspicion that *any* emphasis on 'race' (or other PC favourites such as gender or sexuality) is too much.

Such tactics, however, have only limited potential for engendering the requisite sense of threat and hence the sinister element in PC must be developed. This is achieved partly through portraying an image of social workers as uncaring and callous. While such efforts rely significantly on the 'human interest factor' within particular cases, they are bolstered by reporting of the child care system. Once again, the extraordinary degree of inaccuracy and misrepresentation in reporting raises questions about the motives of those involved. At its crudest, this may involve the assumption that to be in care is synonymous with requiring adoption: 'The aim is to help 40,000 kids in care find new homes' (*Daily Mirror*, 28 August 1998). Numbers in care are also reported in a way which appears to imply 'languishing'. Hugill and Mills (*Observer*, 19 April 1998) describe the number of children in foster care, at 35,000, as 'staggering', yet it has remained fairly constant for decades, while well over half will have entered and/or will leave the care system in any one year.[2] Conspiracy theory reaches its heights when Liv O'Hanlon of the Adoption Forum claims (in an article attacking 'race bans') to have unofficial government information that the true figure for the overall care population is at least 250,000 and probably more (*The Times*, 11 February 1997). Where and how several times the official population could be 'hidden' (and paid for!) within the care system is, to say the least, highly mysterious, as would be the motives for resource-hungry local authorities to under-report their costs on such a scale. Another near constant feature of reporting is that the presumed alternative to adoption is the children's home. Despite the fact that almost all the latter's residents are older and rarely in line for adoption, it is clear that the 'horror' value of foster care is insufficient for audiences.

Equally misreported is the link between PC and adoptable children remaining in care. The undeniably great interest in adoption of babies and young children is uncritically taken as applying to older children and/or those with special needs, an interest being thwarted only by PC: 'New rules will stop the heartache of thousands of couples who want to give loving homes to youngsters but are rejected by politically correct social workers' (*Express on Sunday*, 12 April 1998). The reality of agencies currently struggling to attract interest in older children from prospective adopters is rarely allowed to interrupt the preferred version of events (Collier 1997). The misreporting may also be fuelled by politicians as in Paul Boateng's coupling of the 'excuses' made for rejecting adoptive applicants with the dogma and wrongheadedness about 'keeping families together, no matter what' (*Express on Sunday*, 12 April 1998). Here, he conveniently ignores the fact that homefinding work is almost invariably undertaken by different social workers and only *after* a plan for adoption has been endorsed by the agency and the court, and hence return to family *ruled out*.

The use of 'coded' attacks often associated with liberal racial discourse (Reeves 1983; van Dijk 1993) is also to be found in commentary on adoption. Thus Philpott (1997) talks of social workers 'refusing to place certain kinds of children with certain kinds of substitute parents', while Hugill in 'the shocking case of Jane' (*Observer*, 14 June 1998) argues that 'race' is crucial to it without in any way explaining how. Coded messages are useful for avoiding the need for evidence, and making direct challenge more difficult, but are also designed to be 'read between the lines', allowing innuendo and imagination to create a more powerful effect than would an explicit account. A variant of this technique is to derogate by association with wider, negative imagery. This has included linking the 'violence' of same-race policies with other forms of 'racial violence', as when the *Daily Express* (31 August 1989) linked the forced removal of the child in the Croydon case to violence at the Notting Hill Carnival and anti-Rushdie demonstrations. Similarly, in its demonization of guest Reith lecturer Patricia Williams, the *Daily Mail* chose (wrongly) to emphasize her opposition to TRA as a key marker of her militant black feminism (Karpf 1997).

Chapter 3

1 One of the most striking contemporary examples of this is the defence of Protestant marches through Catholic areas as a rite/right of 'cultural' celebration, conveniently divorced from a history deeply imbued with supremacism and domination.
2 See also Lago (1996: 41–3) on non-verbal communication which takes an ethnicized form.
3 Modood gives the example of celebrations of Black Heroes in the Hall of Fame, all of whom were of African descent (1992: 20).
4 Harris Hendriks and Figueroa (1995) similarly question the appropriateness of the term African–Caribbean when faced with 'island diversity'.

Chapter 4

1 As in other areas of professional practice, there is an important balance to be struck between the detached elitism of 'expertise' on the one hand and crude populism of pandering to 'public opinion' (no matter how well or poorly informed) on the other.
2 It is intended that, dependent on funding, this research will be expanded, ultimately entailing around 40–50 interviews.
3 Interviewees were either members or contacts of ATRAP – the Association of Transracially Adopted People. The latter being a support group, it is plausible to argue that those involved may have found aspects of being transracially adopted more difficult than those not involved. However, it should be emphasized that most members of ATRAP would fit the 'success' criteria widely used in adoption studies, and that there is considerable range in terms of the level of support sought, received and indeed given by members. All names of those interviewed have been changed.
4 The author's own research on attitudes towards 'race' and adoption found very significant differences between white and minority ethnic respondents, especially on issues of racial identity, culture and racism (Kirton 1998). This is hardly surprising if one considers the positioning of white people in relation to racialized discourses and practices i.e. as the invisible centre and beneficiary.

Chapter 5

1 We will be concentrating here on adoption from public care which comprised roughly a third of all adoptions in 1996 (Ivaldi 1998: 8). Other forms of adoption, notably step-parent and other relative adoptions, are not covered here partly due to paucity of information and the more limited role of public agencies. Issues of 'race' and ethnicity can of course be highly contentious in individual cases, most notably when a white parent of a mixed parentage child has married a white partner.
2 Freeing orders were originally introduced in the 1976 Adoption Act as a means of sparing mothers being asked to consent twice to the adoption of their babies. In practice, however, they have been used mainly by local authorities to ask

courts to dispense with parental consent, thereby removing any such obstacle to the eventual adoption application. Particularly in contested proceedings, the term 'freeing' is a highly pejorative one for birth families.

3 It must be remembered that racist rejection of the child by the birth mother's family was often a major factor in relinquishment.

4 This remains the legal position at present, although it was proposed in the 1996 Adoption Bill to replace this test with one based on the welfare of the child.

5 Openness is usually portrayed as operating along a continuum, from the involvement of birth parents in the choice of adopters, via ongoing exchanges of information, letters, cards, phone calls through to face-to-face contact.

6 Less attention has been paid to recruitment of Asian families, partly reflecting the lower numbers of Asian children for whom adoptive homes have been sought and partly the Africanist hegemony within the black radical paradigm. Despite many significant differences, there is much common ground in terms of intercultural (mis)communication, the climate of mistrust between community and agency and so on. See Almas (1992) and Singh (1997) for discussion of work with Asian carers and Yawar (1992) for issues relating more specifically to Muslim children and families.

Chapter 6

1 The account given here is based on the published transcript of the debate.

2 Government statistics on looked after children in England for 1996 show that alongside the snapshot population of 51,200, 31,900 children had started to be looked after during the year and 31,600 ceased to be so.

3 As Marable (1995: 23) observes, there is widespread black belief in white 'double lives', with the racism shown when among other whites hypocritically suppressed when in the company of blacks.

4 Parity, as measured in terms of income and the like, does not necessarily indicate the absence of discrimination or subjection to racism.

5 Taking the labour market as one instance, the past two years have seen a succession of studies and internal enquiries showing continuing discrimination in many major private sector companies, the media, the NHS, the civil service, the judiciary, as well as the old laggards, the police and the army.

6 Especially as an interim measure, the targets could take into account the ethnic composition of areas, with higher targets being set for SSDs based in multiracial areas.

References

ABAA (Association of British Adoption Agencies) (1975) *Adopting a Child: A Brief Guide for Prospective Adopters.* London: Association of British Adoption Agencies.

ABAFA (Association of British Adoption and Fostering Agencies) (1977) *Report on the Soul Kids Campaign.* London: Association of British Adoption and Fostering Agencies.

ABAFA (Association of British Adoption and Fostering Agencies) (1981) Working with West Indian applicants in fostering and adoption: a discussion paper, in J. Cheetham *et al.* (eds) *Social and Community Work in a Multi-racial Society.* London: Harper and Row.

Abdulla, Z. (1998) Listen to me, *Community Care*, 26 March – 1 April, supplement p. 8.

Aboud, F. (1987) The development of ethnic self-identification and attitudes, in J. Phinney and M. Rotheram (eds) *Children's Ethnic Socialisation: Pluralism and Development.* Newbury Park: Sage.

ABSWAP (Association of Black Social Workers and Allied Professionals) (1983) *Black Children in Care: Evidence to the House of Commons Social Services Committee.* London: Association of Black Social Workers and Allied Professionals.

AC (Audit Commission)/SSI (Social Services Inspectorate) (1998) *Getting the Best From Social Services: Learning the Lessons from Joint Reviews.* London: Audit Commission/Department of Health.

Adams, N. (1981) *Black Children in Care.* London: London Borough of Lambeth's Social Services Committee.

ADSS (Association of Directors of Social Services) and CRE (Commission for Racial Equality) (1978) *Multi-racial Britain: The Social Services Response.* London: Commission for Racial Equality.

Ahmed, S. (1981) Children in care: the racial dimension in social work assessment, in J. Cheetham *et al.* (eds) *Social and Community Work in a Multi-racial Society.* London: Harper and Row.

Ahmed, S. (1986) Setting up a community foster action group, in V. Coombe and A. Little (eds) *Race and Social Work.* London: Tavistock.

Akbar, N. (1985) Our destiny: authors of a scientific revolution, in H. McAdoo and J. McAdoo (eds) *Black Children.* Newbury Park: Sage.

Aldridge, J. (1994) In the best interests of the child, in I. Gaber and J. Aldridge (eds) *In the Best Interests of the Child: Culture, Identity and Transracial Adoption.* London: Free Association Books.

Alexander, C. (1996) *The Art of Being Black: the Creation of Black British Youth Identities.* Oxford: Clarendon Press.

Alibhai-Brown, Y. (1997) Bring England in from the cold, *New Statesman,* 11 July, 24–6.

Alibhai-Brown, Y. and Montague, A. (1992) *The Colour of Love: Mixed Race Relationships.* London: Virago.

Allen, N. (1990) *Making Sense of the Children Act 1989,* Harlow: Longman.

Almas, T. (1992) After recruitment: putting the preparation and training of Asian carers on the agenda, *Adoption and Fostering,* 16(3), 25–9.

Altstein, H. and Simon, R. (eds) (1991) *Intercountry Adoption: a Multinational Perspective.* New York: Praeger.

Anderson, B. (1991) *Imagined Communities: Reflections on the Origin and Spread of Nationalism.* London: Verso.

Anthias, F. and Yuval-Davies, N. (1992) *Racialized Boundaries: Race, Nation, Gender, Colour, Class and the Anti-racist Struggle.* London: Routledge.

Anwar, M. (1986) *Race and Politics: Ethnic Minorities and the British Political System.* London: Tavistock.

Anwar, M. (1998) *Ethnic Minorities and the British Electoral System.* Coventry: Centre for Research in Ethnic Relations, University of Warwick.

Argent, H. and Kerrane, A. (1997) *Taking Extra Care: Respite, Shared and Permanent Care for Children with Disabilities.* London: British Agencies for Adoption and Fostering.

Arnold, E. (1982) Finding black families for black children in Britain, in J. Cheetham (ed.) *Social Work and Ethnicity.* London: George Allen and Unwin.

Atherton, C. (1993) Reunification – parallels between placement in new families and reunifying children with their families, in P. Marsh and J. Triseliotis (eds) *Prevention and Reunification in Child Care.* London: Batsford.

Austin, J. (ed.) (1985) *Adoption: the Inside Story.* London: Barn Owl Books.

BAAF (British Agencies for Adoption and Fostering) (1987) *Practice Note 13: The Placement Needs of Black Children.* London: British Agencies for Adoption and Fostering.

Back, L. (1996) *New Ethnicities and Urban Culture: Racisms and Multiculture in Young Lives.* London: UCL Press.

Bagley, C. (1993) *International and Transracial Adoptions: a Mental Health Perspective.* Aldershot: Avebury.

Bagley, C. and Young, L. (1979) The identity, adjustment and achievement of transracially adopted children: a review and empirical report, in G. Verma and C. Bagley (eds) *Race, Education and Identity.* London: Macmillan.

Bagley, C. and Young, L. (1982) Policy dilemmas and the adoption of black children, in J. Cheetham (ed.) *Social Work and Ethnicity.* London: George Allen and Unwin.

Bailey, R. and Brake, M. (eds) (1975) *Radical Social Work.* London: Edward Arnold.

Banks, N. (1992) Techniques for direct identity work with black children, *Adoption and Fostering,* 16(3), 19–25.

Banks, N. (1994) Issues of attachment, separation and identity in contested adoptions, in M. Ryburn (ed.) *Contested Adoptions: Research, Law, Policy and Practice.* Aldershot: Arena.

Feast, J., Marwood, M., Seabrook, S. and Webb, E. (1998) *Preparing for Reunion: Experiences from the Adoption Circle (new edition)*. London: Children's Society.

Feigelman, W. and Silverman, A. (1983) *Chosen Children: New Patterns of Adoptive Relationships*. New York: Praeger.

Feigelman, W. and Silverman, A. (1984) The long-term effects of transracial adoption, *Social Service Review*, December, 588–602.

Fernando, S. (1991) *Mental Health, Race and Culture*. Basingstoke: Macmillan.

Festinger, T. (1990) Adoption disruption: rates and correlates, in D. Brodzinsky and M. Schechter (eds) *The Psychology of Adoption*. New York: Oxford University Press.

Fitzgerald, J. (1981) Black parents for black children, *Adoption and Fostering*, 5(10), 10–11.

Foren, R. and Batta, I. (1970) 'Colour' as a variable in the use made of a local authority child care department, *Social Work*, 27(3), 10–15.

Fox Harding, L. (1991) *Perspectives in Child Care Policy*. London: Longman.

Francis, J. (1992) A shower of love, *Community Care*, 17–23 September, 18–20.

Franklin, A. and Boyd-Franklin, N. (1985) A psychosocial perspective on black parenting, in H. McAdoo and J. McAdoo (eds) *Black Children*. Newbury Park: Sage.

Franklin, B. (1998) *Hard Pressed: National Newspaper Reporting of Social Work and Social Services*. London: Reed Business Information.

Fratter, J. (1996) *Adoption with Contact: Implications for Policy and Practice*. London: British Agencies for Adoption and Fostering.

Fredrickson, G. (1995) *Black Liberation: a Comparative History of Black Ideology in the United States and South Africa*. New York: Oxford University Press.

Freeman, M. (1992) *Children, their Families and the Law: Working with the Children Act*. Basingstoke: Macmillan.

Gaber, I. (1994) Transracial placements in Britain: a history, in I. Gaber and J. Aldridge (eds) *In the Best Interests of the Child: Culture, Identity and Transracial Adoption*. London: Free Association Books.

Gaber, I. and Aldridge, J. (eds) (1994) *In the Best Interests of the Child: Culture, Identity and Transracial Adoption*. London: Free Association Books.

Gabriel, J. (1994) *Racism, Culture, Markets*. London: Routledge.

Gambe, D. (1992) *Improving Practice with Children and Families*. London: Central Council for Education and Training of Social Workers.

Gates, H. (1997) Black flash, *Guardian*, 19 July.

Gates, H. and West, C. (1996) *The Future of the Race*. New York: A.A. Knopf.

George, V. (1970) *Foster Care: Theory and Practice*. London: Routledge and Kegan Paul.

Giddens, A. (1991) *Modernity and Self-Identity: Self and Society in the Late Modern Age*. Cambridge: Polity Press.

Gill, O. and Jackson, B. (1983) *Adoption and Race: Black, Asian and Mixed Race Children in White Families*. London: Batsford.

Gilroy, P. (1987) *There Ain't No Black in the Union Jack*. London: Hutchinson.

Gilroy, P. (1992) The end of anti-racism, in J. Donald and A. Rattansi (eds) *'Race', Culture and Difference*. London: Sage/The Open University.

Gilroy, P. (1993) *The Black Atlantic: Modernity and Double Consciousness*. London: Verso.

Gilroy, P. (1994) Foreword, in I. Gaber and J. Aldridge (eds) *In the Best Interests of the Child: Culture, Identity and Transracial Adoption*. London: Free Association Books.

Glazer, N. and Moynihan, D. (1970) *Beyond the Melting Pot: Puerto Ricans, Jews, Italians, and Irish of New York City*. Cambridge: MIT Press.

Glick, P. (1988) Demographic pictures of black families, in H. McAdoo (ed.) *Black Families*, 2nd edn. Newbury Park: Sage.

Goldberg, D. (1993) *Racist Culture: Philosophy and the Politics of Meaning*. Oxford: Blackwell.

Goldstein, J., Freud, A. and Solnit, A. (1973) *Beyond the Best Interests of the Child*. New York: Free Press.

Golombok, S. (1994) Attachment, in I. Gaber and J. Aldridge (eds) *In the Best Interests of the Child: Culture, Identity and Transracial Adoption*. London: Free Association Books.

Gordon, P. (1983) Medicine, racism and immigration control, *Critical Social Policy*, 7, 6–20.

Gordon, P. (1990) A dirty war: the new right and local authority anti-racism, in W. Ball and J. Solomos (eds) *Race and Local Politics*. London: Macmillan.

Griffith, E. and Silverman, I. (1995) Transracial adoptions and the continuing debate over the racial identity of families, in H. Harris, H. Blue and E. Griffith (eds) *Racial and Ethnic Identity: Psychological Development and Creative Expression*. New York: Routledge.

Groothues, C., Beckett, C. and O'Connor, T. (1998) The outcomes of adoption from Romania: predictors of parental satisfaction, *Adoption and Fostering*, 22(4), 30–40.

Grossberg, L. (1996) Identity and cultural studies: is that all there is?, in S. Hall and P. du Gay (eds) *Questions of Cultural Identity*. London: Sage.

Grow, L. and Shapiro, D. (1974) *Black Children – White Parents: a Study of Transracial Adoption*. New York: Child Welfare League of America.

Haimes, E. and Timms, N. (1985) *Adoption, Identity and Social Policy: the Search for Distant Relatives*. Aldershot: Gower.

Hall, S. (1981) The whites of their eyes: racist ideologies and the media, in G. Bridges and R. Brunt (eds) *Silver Linings*. London: Lawrence and Wishart.

Hall, S. (1990) Cultural identity and diaspora, in J. Rutherford (ed.) *Identity: Community, Culture, Difference*. London: Lawrence and Wishart.

Hall, S. (1996) Introduction: who needs 'identity'?, in S. Hall and P. du Gay (eds) *Questions of Cultural Identity*. London: Sage.

Hall, S., Critcher, C., Jefferson, T., Clarke, J. and Roberts, B. (1978) *Policing the Crisis: Mugging, the State and Law and Order*. London: Macmillan.

Harper, J. (1994) Counselling issues in intercountry adoption disruption, *Adoption and Fostering*, 18(2), 20–6.

Harris, K. (1985) *Transracial Adoption: a Bibliography*. London: British Agencies for Adoption and Fostering.

Harris Hendriks, J. and Figueroa, J. (1995) *Black in White: the Caribbean Child in the UK Home*. London: Pitman.

Harrison, A. (1985) The black family's socialising environment: self-esteem and ethnic attitude among black children, in H. McAdoo and J. McAdoo (eds) *Black Children*. Newbury Park: Sage.

Hauser, S. (1971) *Black and White Identity Formation: Studies in the Psychosocial Development of Lower Socioeconomic Class Adolescent Boys*. New York: John Wiley.

Hayes, M. (1996a) Post-adoption issues in transracial adoptions and same race placements, in R. Phillips and E. McWilliam (eds) *After Adoption: Working with Adoptive Families*. London: British Agencies for Adoption and Fostering.

Hayes, M. (1996b) Transracial adopted people's support group, in R. Phillips and E. McWilliam (eds) *After Adoption: Working with Adoptive Families*. London: British Agencies for Adoption and Fostering.

Heller, M. (1987) The role of language in the formation of ethnic identity, in J. Phinney and M. Rotheram (eds) *Children's Ethnic Socialisation: Pluralism and Development*. Newbury Park: Sage.

Heywood (1990) Putting same-race placement into practice, *Adoption and Fostering*, 14(2), 9–10.

Hewitt, R. (1986) *White Talk, Black Talk: Inter-racial Friendship and Communication amongst Adolescents*. Cambridge: Cambridge University Press.

Hibbs, E. (1991) *Adoption: International Perspectives*. Madison: International Universities Press.

Hill, M. (1991) Concepts of parenthood and their application to adoption, *Adoption and Fostering*, 15(4), 16–23.

Hill, M., Lambert, L. and Triseliotis, J. (1989) *Achieving Adoption with Love and Money*. London: National Children's Bureau.

Hill Collins, P. (1990) *Black Feminist Thought*. Boston: Unwin Hyman.

Hills, R. (1971) *The Strengths of Black Families*. Washington: National Urban League.

Hiro, D. (1973) *Black British, White British*. Harmondsworth: Pelican.

Hoch, P. (1979) *White Hero, Black Beast: Racism, Sexism and the Mask of Masculinity*. London: Pluto.

Hollingsworth, L. (1998) Adoptee dissimilarity from the adoptive family: clinical practice and research implications, *Child and Adolescent Social Work Journal*, 15(4), 303–19.

Holman, R. (1978) A class analysis of adoption reveals a disturbing picture, *Community Care*, 26 April, 30.

Holmes, C. (1991) *A Tolerant Country? Immigrants, Refugees and Minorities in Britain*. London: Faber and Faber.

Home Office Advisory Council on Child Care (1970) *A Guide to Adoption Practice*. London: HMSO.

hooks, b. (1992) *Black Looks: Race and Representation*. London: Turnaround.

Hoopes, J. (1990) Adoption and identity formation, in D. Brodzinsky and M. Schechter (eds) *The Psychology of Adoption*. New York: Oxford University Press.

Howe, D. and Hinings, D. (1987) Adopted children referred to a child and family centre, *Adoption and Fostering*, 11(3), 44–7.

Howe, D., Sawbridge, P. and Hinings, D. (1992) *Half a Million Women: Mothers Who Lose their Children by Adoption*. London: Penguin.

Husain, M. and Husain, S. (1996) Mix 'n match, in R. Phillips and E. McWilliam (eds) *After Adoption: Working with Adoptive Families*. London: British Agencies for Adoption and Fostering.

Husain Sumpton, A. (1999) Communicating with and assessing black children, in R. Barn (ed.) *Working with Black Children and Adolescents in Need*. London: British Agencies for Adoption and Fostering.

Husband, C. (1980) Culture, context and practice: racism in social work, in M. Brake and R. Bailey (eds) *Radical Social Work and Practice*. London: Edward Arnold.

Ince, L. (1998) *Making It Alone: a Study of the Care Experiences of Young Black People*. London: British Agencies for Adoption and Fostering.

Independent Adoption Society (1975) *Annual Report*. London: Independent Adoption Society.

Inglis, K. (1984) *Living Mistakes: Mothers Who Consented to Adoption*. Sydney: Allen & Unwin.

Inman, K. (1998) Cold comfort, *Community Care*, 26 November – 2 December, 9.

Ivaldi, G. (1998) *Children Adopted from Care: an Examination of Agency Adoptions in England – 1996*. London: British Agencies for Adoption and Fostering.

Jackson, B. (1976) *Family Exeriences of Inter-racial Adoption*. London: Association of British Adoption Agencies.

Jackson, J., McCullough, W. and Gurin, G. (1988) Family, socialisation environment, and identity development in black Americans, in H. McAdoo (ed.) *Black Families*, 2nd edn. Newbury Park: Sage.

James, M. (1986) Finding and working with families of Caribbean origin, in V. Coombe and A. Little (eds) *Race and Social Work*. London: Tavistock.

James, W. (1981) Working with children and families – introduction, in J. Cheetham *et al.* (eds) *Social and Community Work in a Multi-racial Society*. London: Harper and Row.

Jenkins, R. (1997) *Rethinking Ethnicity: Arguments and Explorations*. London: Sage.

Jenkins, S. (1982) The American ethnic dilemma, in J. Cheetham (ed.) *Social Work and Ethnicity*. London: George Allen and Unwin.

John, G. (1972) The social worker and the young blacks, in J. Triseliotis (ed.) *Social Work with Coloured Immigrants and their Families*. London: Oxford University Press.

Johnson, L. (1988) Perspectives on black family empirical research 1965–1978, in H. McAdoo (ed.) *Black Families*, 2nd edn. Newbury Park: Sage.

Johnson, M. (1991) Race, Social Work and Child Care, in P. Carter, T. Jeffs and M. Smith (eds) *Social Work and Social Welfare Yearbook 3*. Buckingham: Open University Press.

Johnson, P., Shireman, J. and Watson, K. (1987) Transracial adoption and the development of black identity at age eight, *Child Welfare*, 66(1), 45–55.

Jones, A. (1998) *The Child Welfare Implications of UK Immigration and Asylum Policy*. Manchester: Manchester Metropolitan University.

Jones, C. (1977) *Immigration and Social Policy in Britain*. London: Tavistock.

Jones, C. and Else, J. (1979) Racial and cultural issues in adoption, *Child Welfare*, 58(6), 373–82.

Jordan, B. (1994) Contested adoptions and the role of the state in family matters, in M. Ryburn (ed.) *Contested Adoptions: Research, Law, Policy and Practice*. Aldershot: Arena.

Kaniuk, J. (1991) Strategies in recruiting black adopters, *Adoption and Fostering*, 15(1), 38–42.

Karpf, A. (1997) Fighting talk, *Guardian*, 23 January.

Katz, I. (1996) *The Construction of Racial Identity in Children of Mixed Parentage: Mixed Metaphors*. London: Jessica Kingsley.

Kelly, C., Clare, S. and Stober, J. (1989) Black issues in child care – training for foster carers and adoptive parents, *Adoption and Fostering*, 13(3), 29–33.

Kelly, G. and Coulter, J. (1997) The Children (Northern Ireland) Order 1995, *Adoption and Fostering*, 21(3), 5–13.

Kent, B. (1972) The social worker's cultural pattern as it affects casework with immigrants, in J. Triseliotis (ed.) *Social Work with Coloured Immigrants and their Families*. Oxford: Oxford University Press.

Rutherford, J. (1990) A place called home: identity and the cultural politics of difference, in J. Rutherford (ed.) *Identity: Community, Culture, Difference.* London: Lawrence and Wishart.

Ryburn, M. (1992) Contested adoption proceedings, *Adoption and Fostering*, 16(4), 29–38.

Ryburn, M. (ed.) (1994a) *Contested Adoptions: Research, Law, Policy and Practice.* Aldershot: Arena.

Ryburn, M. (1994b) *Open Adoption: Research, Theory and Practice.* Aldershot: Avebury.

Ryburn, M. (1994c) Contested adoption: the perspective of birth parents, in M. Ryburn (ed.) *Contested Adoptions: Research, Law, Policy and Practice.* Aldershot: Arena.

Ryburn, M. (1994d) The use of an adversarial process in contested adoptions, in M. Ryburn (ed.) *Contested Adoptions: Research, Law, Policy and Practice.* Aldershot: Arena.

Saggar, S. (1992) *Race and Politics in Britain.* Hemel Hempstead: Harvester Wheatsheaf.

Sarup, M. (1993) *An Introductory Guide to Post-structuralism and Post-modernism.* Hemel Hempstead: Harvester Wheatsheaf.

Save the Children (1997) *Private Fostering: Development of Policy and Practice in Three English Local Authorities.* London: Save the Children.

Sawbridge, P. (1988) The post adoption centre – what are the users teaching us?, *Adoption and Fostering*, 12(1), 5–12.

Scarman, L. (1982) *The Scarman Report: the Brixton Disorders, 10–12 April 1981.* Harmondsworth: Pelican.

Schechter, M. and Bertocci, D. (1990) The meaning of the search, in D. Brodzinsky and M. Schechter (eds) *The Psychology of Adoption.* New York: Oxford University Press.

Schroeder, H. and Lightfoot, D. (1983) Finding black families, *Adoption and Fostering*, 7(1), 18–21.

Selwyn, J. (1996) Ascertaining children's wishes and feelings in relation to adoption, *Adoption and Fostering*, 20(3), 14–20.

Shawyer, J. (1979) *Death by Adoption.* Auckland: Cicada Press.

Shotter, J. (1989) Social accountability and the social construction of 'you', in J. Shotter and K. Gergen (eds) *Texts of Identity.* London: Sage.

Simon, R. (1994) Transracial adoption: the American experience, in I. Gaber and J. Aldridge (eds) *In the Best Interests of the Child: Culture, Identity and Transracial Adoption.* London: Free Association Books.

Simon, R. and Altstein, H. (1977) *Transracial Adoption.* New York: Wiley.

Simon, R. and Altstein, H. (1987) *Transracial Adoptees and their Families: a Study of Identity and Commitment.* New York: Praeger.

Simon, R., Altstein, H. and Melli, M. (1994) *The Case for Transracial Adoption.* Washington, DC: American University Press.

Singh, S. (1997) Assessing Asian families in Scotland: a discussion, *Adoption and Fostering*, 21(3), 35–9.

Sivanandan, A. (1982) *A Different Hunger: Writings on Black Resistance.* London: Pluto.

Skellington, R. (1996) *'Race' in Britain.* Buckingham: Open University Press.

Slugowski, B. and Ginsburg, G. (1989) Ego identity and explanatory speech, in J. Shotter and K. Gergen (eds) *Texts of Identity.* London: Sage.

Small, J. (1982) New black families, *Adoption and Fostering*, 6(3), 35–9.

Small, J. (1986) Transracial placements: conflicts and contradictions, in S. Ahmed, J. Cheetham and J. Small (eds) *Social Work with Black Children and their Families*. London: Batsford.

Small, J. (1991) Ethnic and racial identity in adoption within the United Kingdom, *Adoption and Fostering*, 15(4), 61–8.

Small, S. (1994) *Racialised Barriers: the Black Experience in the United States and England in the 1980s*. London: Routledge.

Smith, C. (1993) Restoring children from foster care to their parents, in P. Marsh and J. Triseliotis (eds) *Prevention and Reunification in Child Care*. London: Batsford.

Smith, D. (1977) *Racial Disadvantage in Britain*. Harmondsworth: Penguin.

Solomos, J. (1993) *Race and Racism in Britain*, 2nd edn. Basingstoke: Macmillan.

Spencer, M. (1987) Black children's ethnic identity formation: risk and resilience of castelike minorities, in J. Phinney and M. Rotheram (eds) *Children's Ethnic Socialisation: Pluralism and Development*. Newbury Park: Sage.

SSI (Social Services Inspectorate) (1990) *Letter No. CI(90)2*. London: Department of Health.

SSI (Social Services Inspectorate) (1993) *Planning for Permanence: Adoption Services in Three Northern Local Authorities*. London: Department of Health.

SSI (Social Services Inspectorate) (1996a) *Letter No. CI(96)4*. London: Department of Health.

SSI (Social Services Inspectorate) (1996b) *For Children's Sake: an SSI Inspection of Local Authority Adoption Services*. London: Department of Health.

SSI (Social Services Inspectorate) (1997) *For Children's Sake, Part 2: an Inspection of Local Authority Post-placement and Post-adoption Services*. London: Department of Health.

Stewart, J. and Stoker, G. (eds) (1989) *The Future of Local Government*. Basingstoke: Macmillan.

Stuart, A. (1990) Feminism: dead or alive?, in J. Rutherford (ed.) *Identity, Community, Culture, Difference*. London: Lawrence and Wishart.

Stubbs, P. (1987) Professionalism and the adoption of black children, *British Journal of Social Work*, 17, 473–92.

Tatum, B. (1997) Out there stranded? Black families in white communities, in H. McAdoo (ed.) *Black Families*, 3rd edn. Thousand Oaks: Sage.

Thoburn, J. (1991) Survey findings and conclusions, in J. Fratter, J. Rowe, R. Sapsford and J. Thoburn. *Permanent Family Placement: a Decade of Experience*. London: British Agencies for Adoption and Fostering.

Thompson, A. (1996) Black and white, *Community Care*, 23–29 May, 14–15.

Thompson, A. (1997) Black power, *Community Care*, 24–30 July, 18–19.

Thorpe, D. (1994) *Evaluating Child Protection*. Buckingham: Open University Press.

Tingle, N. (1994) A view of wider family perspectives in contested adoptions, in M. Ryburn (ed.) *Contested Adoptions: Research, Law, Policy and Practice*. Aldershot: Arena.

Tizard, B. (1977) *Adoption: a Second Chance*. London: Open Books.

Tizard, B. (1991) Intercountry adoption: a review of the evidence, *Journal of Child Psychology and Psychiatry*, 32(5), 743–56.

Tizard, B. and Pheonix, A. (1989) Black identity and transracial adoption, *New Community*, 15, 427–38.

Tizard, B. and Pheonix, A. (1993) *Black, White or Mixed Race? Race and Racism in the Lives of Young People of Mixed Parentage*. London: Routledge.

Tizard, B. and Pheonix, A. (1994) Black identity and transracial adoption, in I. Gaber and J. Aldridge (eds) *In the Best Interests of the Child: Culture, Identity and Transracial Adoption*. London: Free Association Books.

Toor, K. (1997) Find me a family: the black perspective, unpublished MA dissertation, University of Kent.

Triseliotis, J. (1972) The implications of cultural factors in social work with immigrants, in J. Triseliotis (ed.) *Social Work with Coloured Immigrants and their Families*. Oxford: Oxford University Press.

Triseliotis, J. (ed.) (1988) *Groupwork in Adoption and Foster Care*. London: Batsford.

Triseliotis, J. (1991a) Perceptions of permanence, *Adoption and Fostering*, 15(4), 6–15.

Triseliotis, J. (1991b) Open adoption, in A. Mullender (ed.) *Open Adoption: the Philosophy and Practice*. London: British Agencies for Adoption and Fostering.

Triseliotis, J., Sellick, C. and Short, R. (1995) *Foster Care: Theory and Practice*. London: Batsford.

Triseliotis, J., Shireman, J. and Hundleby, M. (1997) *Adoption: Theory, Policy and Practice*. London: Cassell.

Ussher, J. (1991) *Women's Madness: Misogyny or Mental Illness*. Hemel Hemptstead: Harvester Wheatsheaf.

Valios, N. (1996) Social workers ignore new government adoption plans, *Community Care*, 11–17 April, 4–5.

Van de Flier Davis, D. (1995) Capitalising on adoption, *Adoption and Fostering*, 19(2), 25–30.

van Dijk, T. (1993) *Elite Discourse and Racism*. Newbury Park: Sage.

Vyas, I. (1993) Openness in adoption: some concerns, in M. Adcock, J. Kaniuk and R. White (eds) *Exploring Openness in Adoption*. Croydon: Significant Publications.

Wade Boykin, A. and Toms, F. (1985) Black child socialisation: a conceptual framework, in H. McAdoo and J. McAdoo (eds) *Black Children*. Newbury Park: Sage.

Waterhouse, S. (1997) *The Organisation of Fostering Services: a Study of the Arrangements for Delivery of Fostering Services in England*. London: National Foster Care Association.

Waters, M. (1990) *Ethnic Options: Choosing Identities in America*. Berkeley: University of California Press.

Weise, J. (1988) *Transracial adoption: a black perspective*, Social Work Monographs 60. Norwich: University of East Anglia.

Wellman, D. (1993) *Portraits of White Racism*, 2nd edn. Cambridge: Cambridge University Press.

Wells, S. (1993) What do Birthmothers Want?, *Adoption and Fostering*, 17(4), 22–6.

Wetherell, M. and Potter, J. (1992) *Mapping the Language of Racism: Discourse and the Legitimation of Exploitation*. Hemel Hempstead: Harvester Wheatsheaf.

White, H. (1985) *Black Children, White Adopters: an Exploration in Uncertainty*, Social Work Monograph 31. Norwich: University of East Anglia.

Wilkinson, A. (1982) *Children who Come into Care in Tower Hamlets*. London: London Borough of Tower Hamlets.

Williams, C. (1974) *The Destruction of Black Civilisation: Great Issues of a Race from 4500 BC to 2000 AD*. Chicago: Third World Press.

Wilson, A. (1987) *Mixed Race Children: a Study of Identity*. London: Unwin Hyman.

Wilson, C. (1996) *Racism: from Slavery to Advanced Capitalism*. Thousand Oaks: Sage.

Winkler, R. and Van Keppel, M. (1984) *Relinquishing Mothers in Adoption: Their Long-term Adjustment*. Melbourne: Institute of Family Studies.

Yawar, T. (1992) *Caring about Faith: Report of a Survey of Muslim Children and Young Persons in Care*. Leicester: The Islamic Foundation.

Yaya, B. (1994) *Transracial Fostering – a Black Perspective*, Social Work Monographs 130. Norwich: University of East Anglia.

Young, K. (1983) Ethnic pluralism and the policy agenda in Britain, in N. Glazer and K. Young (eds) *Ethnic Pluralism and Public Policy: Achieving Equality in the United States and Britain*. London: Heinemann.

Young, R. (1990) *White Mythologies: Writing History and the West*. London: Routledge

Young, K. and Connelly, N. (1981) *Policy and Practice in the Multi-racial City*. London: Policy Studies Institute.

Younge, G. (1994) Mixed blessings, *Guardian*, 6 December.

Zeitlin, H. (1996) Adoption of children from minority groups, in K. Dwiwedi and V. Varma (eds) *Meeting the Needs of Ethnic Minority Children: a Handbook for Professionals*. London: Jessica Kingsley.

Zubaida, S. (1970) (ed.) *Race and Racialism*. London: Tavistock.

Index

Reeves, F., 124, 127
religion, 52
  see also Muslims, British
Rhodes, P., 25, 114, 115, 122
Richards, B., 33, 41, 42
Robinson, L., 61, 68
Rosenblatt, P., 55, 56
Ryburn, M., 2, 109–10

self-esteem, 35–6
  and racial identity, 36–41, 65–6
separate organization/separatism, 24,
  85, 121–2, 131
Simon, R., 39, 40, 121
Simon, R. and Altstein, H., 9, 16, 34,
  35, 37, 44, 46, 48, 49, 51, 120
Small, J., 22, 62–3, 69, 70, 72, 73
Small, S., 4, 12, 22, 121

social class, 49–50
  liberal middle class and transracial
  adoption (TRA), 9, 32
social mobility through adoption, 2
Social Services Inspectorate (SSI), 30,
  117
Soul Kids Campaign, 18
Stubbs, P., 62, 113, 114, 115

Tizard, B., 16, 105
Tizard, B. and Pheonix, A., 41, 73, 98,
  134
Triseliotis, J., 18, 41

van Dijk, T., 127

Wade Boykin, A. and Toms, F., 71
Waters, M., 87